251 STUDY SECRETS from the Diary of a TOP ACHIEVER

Excel in studies and ensure success in exams & career

B.K. Narayan
&
Preeti Narayan

V&S PUBLISHERS

Published by:

F-2/16, Ansari Road, Daryaganj, New Delhi-110002
011-23240026, 011-23240027 • *Fax:* 011-23240028
Email: info@vspublishers.com • *Website:* www.vspublishers.com

Branch : Hyderabad
5-1-707/1, Brij Bhawan (Beside Central Bank of India Lane)
Bank Street, Koti, Hyderabad - 500 095
040-24737290
E-mail: vspublishershyd@gmail.com

Follow us on:

For any assistance sms **VSPUB** to **56161**

All books available at **www.vspublishers.com**

© **Copyright: Author**
ISBN 978-93-813847-9-4
Edition 2013

The Copyright of this book, as well as all matter contained herein (including illustrations) rests with the Publishers. No person shall copy the name of the book, its title design, matter and illustrations in any form and in any language, totally or partially or in any distorted form. Anybody doing so shall face legal action and will be responsible for damages.

Printed at : Param Offsetters, Okhla, New Delhi-110020

Contents

Preface	7
○ *Chapter 1*	
4 Self-Motivation Secrets to Study Better	9
○ *Chapter 2*	
6 Secrets to Boost Confidence	11
○ *Chapter 3*	
13 Secrets to Choose Your Career Goal	15
○ *Chapter 4*	
9 Secrets to Fix Goals in Your Mind	24
○ *Chapter 5*	
6 Secrets to Boost Brainpower	29
○ *Chapter 6*	
8 Secrets to Programme Yourself for Success	33
○ *Chapter 7*	
10 Secrets to Attain 100% Concentration	38
○ *Chapter 8*	
9 Secrets to Manage Your Time Efficiently	44
○ *Chapter 9*	
8 Secrets to Become More Energetic	49
○ *Chapter 10*	
10 Secrets to be on Good Terms with Your Teacher!	53
○ *Chapter 11*	
12 Secrets to Learn More in Class	58
○ *Chapter 12*	
10 Secrets to Take Better Notes In Class	63
○ *Chapter 13*	
13 Secrets to Take Detailed Notes	67

- *Chapter 14*
  - **6 Secrets to Maintain Good Relations with Classmates**   72
- *Chapter 15*
  - **6 Secrets to Choose a Good Tutor**   75
- *Chapter 16*
  - **7 Secrets to Make Your Study Place Perfect**   77
- *Chapter 17*
  - **6 Secrets to Read Faster and Understand Better**   80
- *Chapter 18*
  - **13 Secrets to Study Better and Smarter**   83
- *Chapter 19*
  - **2 Secrets to Revise Effectively**   88
- *Chapter 20*
  - **5 Secrets to Solve Maths Problems**   90
- *Chapter 21*
  - **11 Secrets to Multiply Memory Power**   92
- *Chapter 22*
  - **8 Secrets to Make Difficult Subjects Easy**   98
- *Chapter 23*
  - **4 Secrets to Clear Backlog Quickly**   102
- *Chapter 24*
  - **4 Secrets to Public Speaking**   104
- *Chapter 25*
  - **7 Secrets to Excel in Exams and Tests**   106
- *Chapter 26*
  - **11 Secrets to Write Perfect Answers in Exams**   110
- *Chapter 27*
  - **12 Secrets to Make Your Exam Day Perfect**   114
- *Chapter 28*
  - **14 Secrets to Combat Stress**   120
- *Chapter 29*
  - **11 Secrets to Prevent Problems**   126
- *Chapter 30*
  - **6 Master Secrets to be *More* Successful**   131

How to get best results from this book

1. Methods given in this book are useful for students from school to university level. Students below 12 years will need parental **help** in using these methods.
2. To begin with, **read all the 251 Secrets once**. While reading, mark those you feel are important.
3. For *permanent* improvement, use the methods you find important *repeatedly*. Remember, we learn everything by repetition. Once you finish learning the important methods, start using these *till they become your new habits*.
4. Read Master Mind Programme *EVERYDAY*, till you reach your goal.
5. Fill up and use *Career Goal Card* and *Subject-wise Target Card*. Read these cards everyday till you reach your goal.
6. To find methods to deal with a particular problem, refer to the *Table of Contents*.
7. If you think a particular step or method needs more explanation, keep reading further, then return to the problem section. You will understand it better.

Amazing Secrets About Yourself

We have not met each other, yet I know a few things about you that you yourself may not!

Here's what I know about you:

- ✦ You are a born winner.
- ✦ You are strong.
- ✦ You are intelligent.
- ✦ You have already achieved many significant things.
- ✦ You have the ability to achieve anything you really want by making effective use of your UNLIMITED brainpower.

Can't believe this? Then visit our website: **www.mindpowerguide.biz** for a FREE copy of the first chapter of *SUCCESS MINDWARE for Complete Development of Students* and use it as instructed. Your doubts will be dispelled once you begin achieving significant success easily.

—B.K. Narayan

Preface

Dear friend,

Thank you for investing in this book.

This book includes practical **methods to make education and examination easy for you.** These methods have worked for many students and will work for you too.

When I was a student years ago, I had failed in an exam. Then accidentally, I used just one method—looking at my 'target-score' daily until I achieved it. This single method transformed me from a failure into a successful student. Then onwards, I passed every exam with top grades.

—*B. K. Narayan*

This proves that even a *single* idea or strategy, if followed *consistently*, can transform a student's performance and direction in life.

Can you imagine what happens when you apply a whole *set of powerful* methods given in this book? These techniques have transformed under-performers into top performers. *Now is your turn.*

Till 7th standard I was an average student. Then, luckily, my parents introduced me to Mind Programming and better study techniques. Ever since, learning fast and scoring high became my habit.

I have included many methods in this book that helped me achieve brilliant academic success. Now you too can use these powerful techniques to reach the top. And stay there!

—*Preeti Narayan*

Use information in this book to become a **top achiever**.

Good luck! Fly beyond your dreams!!

B.K. Narayan

&

Preeti Narayan

Authors

http://www.mindpowerguide.biz

CHAPTER 1

4 Self-Motivation Secrets to Study Better

1. Always remember that someday you will need to show your report card to important people.

Some of those will be:
- Admission authorities of institutions
- Your employer
- Your business partner
- Your life partner
- Your children

Imagine how you would feel before them if your grades or marks were low. Uncomfortable! How about your chance of clearing that interview? Slim! And how motivating would it be for your children once you were a parent? Un-motivating!

So what must you choose now? ONLY TOP SUCCESS! Yes, only top success in your studies.

Don't worry; you can make it. *This is a simple job for that super-computer—your brain.* All you need do is use the secrets in this book.

2. Make a list of all the things and benefits you will *lose* if you have poor grades or marks.

Many students do not realize the magnitude of their loss when they study poorly. This list will be an eye-opener. To prepare this list, use any diary or notebook and write down the losses you will suffer if you get poor grades.

Here are six examples of such losses to drive home the point:
- Loss of confidence and self-esteem
- Little respect in society—people love and respect only winners!
- Low income
- Stressful life
- Poor or lower middle-class lifestyle
- Marriage to an ordinary boy or a plain Jane!

Many who neglected studies in their teens are now living a life of frustration. To confirm this, just consider your relatives and friends. You will be surprised at what you find.

So take a conscious decision right now NOT to live such a low-quality life and aim for absolute success in studies. Shoulder the responsibility of creating the future you will enjoy.

Remember, ONLY YOU can control your future.

3. **List the multiple advantages of studying well and obtaining good grades.**

We all love to do things that ensure benefits and advantages. You will be more interested in studies if you are aware of the huge advantages you will enjoy if you study well.

So if you hate studies or begin to feel bored, just read this list of advantages. Your hatred or boredom will evaporate and your mind will be **charged** to study more.

Below are five illustrative benefits of studying well. Read them. Then note down other benefits you can obtain by studying well:

- Greater confidence
- Higher self-esteem
- Better career or business opportunities
- Happy parents and teachers
- Eligibility for Scholarships and other awards

List more benefits that are important to you. For example: visiting beautiful places, owning a car, living in a luxurious bungalow, etc.

4. **Meet people who have completed their education with good grades and are now enjoying their dream career or lifestyle.**

Such meetings will make you yearn for success! You will also feel the desire to study well and enjoy life like them.

Ask them relevant questions, like:

- What qualifications and skills must you acquire to become like them or to enter and succeed in their field?
- How did they prepare for their exams?
- By the time you complete your education will there still be demand in their field?
- Are they enjoying their career and profession?
- How is their personal life now? Do they find enough leisure time with family and friends?

∞

CHAPTER 2

6 Secrets to Boost Confidence

1. **Always have a SUCCESSFUL SELF IMAGE in mind, no matter how poor your present performance.**

   + Want a fabulous report card?
     First visualize it in your mind.
   + Want to become a doctor?
     Then visualize it in your mind.
   + Want unlimited success?
     Visualize it in your mind.

   Don't forget—everything starts in your mind. Everything starts with your thoughts. If you want success, always visualize yourself as a *successful person*. Hold a positive self-image about yourself.

   Your confidence will then automatically increase. And you will find it easier to achieve success.

   Indeed, this is the secret of bright students: they always consider themselves winners. So it becomes easy for them to *think and do* things that take them to their goal—of achieving TOP success in studies. Now you too can achieve big-time success. Just GO for it!

2. **List the good marks or grades you have scored in your entire educational life till now. You can also write down good remarks made by your teachers.**

   Open your old school or college records. Against each subject, find the good marks you have scored. Copy them in your diary. If your teacher praises you in class, include it in this list along with the date!

   Give some motivating name to this list, like:

   'My Amazing Scores List'
   or
   'Proof of Being A Good Student'

   Look at this list closely whenever you feel low or think you are a poor student. You will instantly feel a burst of confidence.

   Frequently reading this list helps you develop the habit of thinking "I CAN ACHIEVE ANYTHING." Such thinking increases your confidence, makes you more positive and helps you to use your brainpower efficiently.

This is a SMART way to achieve success—allowing your brain to work smoothly without negative thoughts draining it. Therefore, while making this list, ignore poor results!

3. Keep repeating, "I have unlimited brainpower. I can learn anything. I am a brilliant student."

This technique of giving positive suggestions to ourselves is called Self-suggestion, Affirmation or Autosuggestion.

Mentally repeat the above sentences five times daily. This simple act of repeating positive affirmations increases your confidence. When you *continue* using positive affirmations another big change will occur in you—as a wonderful side effect…

> *You will automatically cultivate*
> *a **most important success-habit**—*
> *paying more attention to your strengths*
> *and ignoring weaknesses.*

So start using the above affirmations. You will discover more powerful affirmations in this book to improve other important areas of your student life.

You can repeat these sentences before starting your studies, while sitting in class, before going to bed and after getting up in the morning.

Don't ignore this method because it seems so simple. This method works because it utilizes a powerful truth: *you get what you think repeatedly*. And affirmations help you to repeatedly think about positive thoughts, which help to bring about powerful changes in you.

4. Here's an excellent confidence booster. Mentally repeat this affirmation several times a day: "*I have a perfect brain and by using this perfect brain, I can be a genius in my chosen field.*"

Don't be scared by the word 'genius'. Remember what Thomas Alva Edison said:

> **"Genius is 1% inspiration**
> **and 99% perspiration."**

If you can read, comprehend, and remember what you are reading now, then you have a perfect brain. For a perfect brain, 1% inspiration is child's play. And we will teach you how to perspire!

Also know that genius is NOT:

✦ Scoring 100 per cent in every subject
✦ Winning an Olympic medal in all sports

- Being the world's wealthiest person
- Becoming an expert in everything

To be a genius you need not be any of these. A genius means being...

Being the best in just one field—your chosen field, like teaching, drawing performing surgery etc.

This is easy for your powerful brain. Just learn how to use your brainpower correctly.

5. Prepare your SUCCESS List.

This is the greatest favour you can do yourself.

If this is done, you can use the Success List to programme your brain to automatically focus on thoughts and actions that *lead you to success.*

We have been programmed in early childhood to *almost always* think about our weaknesses, mistakes, and drawbacks. To be successful, you need to delete this early programming. The Success List helps you to do this easily.

As the name suggests, the Success List is just that, a list of all your big, small and even silly successes.

For instance: painting a nice picture, writing neatly, a good score in spellings, various exams passed, games won, speeches given, or any other skills or things that you have done and are good at.

The Success List makes you aware of your strengths and helps you *focus more* on your good qualities and successes. So take a diary and list all your little and big achievements. And always keep adding to the list!

DO THIS NOW!

Once you list your successes, the next thing to DO is to look at your list *daily* and say, *"If I can achieve all these, I can Achieve More!"*

6. KNOW that you are a Born Winner, and can continue to be a winner.

With this belief, you can move mountains. When you believe that you are a born winner and can continue to win in life, you will develop a *"I Can Achieve Anything"* mindset.

This kind of positive mindset gives you the power to think big, act smart and achieve all your dreams.

So always think, "I am a born winner," and "I can achieve anything." If you want more help in this regard visit our website www.mindpowerguide.biz where you will receive FREE training to develop strong self-confidence and to start achieving more success in life. You will also receive proof on how you are a born winner. You will get all this and much more for FREE, so go for it.

You need an Internet connection to get this free help. If you don't have this facility at home, use the one at your school or college or find a friend who has one. Or you can visit an Internet café along with a friend.

But don't let "excuses" prevent you from using this free help!

∞

CHAPTER 3

13 Secrets to Choose Your Career Goal

1. Choose your career goal NOW.

A career goal answers your *'WHY should I study'* question.

This answer helps you realize that studying is a path to your destination—your dream career. Walk on this path properly and you will definitely reach your destination and live happily too.

Besides, research has shown that students who choose career goals early score better grades and have fewer academic problems.

Why this is so? Simply because, when you choose a career goal of *your choice* you feel a strong desire to achieve it. This desire ensures you love your studies. When you *love* your studies, 50 per cent of your study problems are automatically solved! You can solve the rest by using this book.

Once you choose your career goal, do a smart thing: *List all the small and big benefits you get when you realize your career dream.* Check this list frequently or whenever you lack the desire to study.

2. Visualize how you want to live your life.

If you are yet to decide a career goal, don't worry. You can use the exercise given below to choose the right career goal.

This exercise is based on the following principle: a lot of information is stored in your brain. In this huge storehouse of information, there is information related to your career goal also—hidden in the form of your reactions to stories you heard, the experiences of others, movies you saw, books and articles you read about different careers, etc.

When you do this exercise, your brain checks its vast storehouse of information and gives you hints to choose the right career.

Follow these simple steps: Close your eyes. Let your mind run wild and imagine...

✦ How do you want to live your life?

- ✦ What kind of job do you want?
- ✦ Imagine yourself in detail in each of the career options you are considering.

Do this for 15-20 minutes. Open your eyes slowly, and ask yourself, "Which career can I enjoy most?" Note the answer you receive. If you do not get a satisfactory answer, try this exercise again after a few days.

3. **Your goals should be high enough to inspire you and realistic enough to be achieved.**

While setting any goal, be judicious. Do not set goals that are too easy—ordinary goals do not motivate. Also do not set goals that are too difficult. You might feel overwhelmed and give up midway.

The best trick is to start with goals that seem near, but are far enough to make you jump to reach them. Challenging, isn't it?

Now, do not worry about whether you will be able to achieve the academic or career goal that you set.

Just set your goal and start trying to achieve it. Remember, no one is born with a particular skill or ability. Everyone has to **develop** specific skills and abilities after coming into this world.

Also, here's a special tip—you can develop any skill or ability you need to achieve success in your career goal by using three strategies:

- ✦ Using your brainpower to master a skill.
- ✦ Learning a particular skill from people who are good at it.
- ✦ Using that skill *repeatedly till you become an expert in it.*

4. **Ensure your goals are specific and clear.**

Your brain does not work properly when it receives confusing orders. Your brain will help you focus on your goal only when it is *specific*.

It is like saying, "I want to enjoy my summer holidays in a foreign country." Foreign country? Okay, but where? Without being specific, how can you book tickets, make travel plans and organise reservations? It just does not work.

It is the same with your career. If you are not specific in choosing your career goal, you cannot be motivated *enough* to succeed.

Now you might say, "I am so young. I am still studying. How can I be specific in choosing my career?" Okay friend, you think it is a genuine excuse. But, sorry! You must still choose a specific career goal. Why? Simply because *only* a specific goal can *influence* you to think and act like a brilliant student.

Besides, you can change your career goal *later* if you find a better one! Got it?

Now, what is your specific goal? Did you say, "I want to be an engineer?" This is still not specific enough. But if you say, "I want to be a Software Engineer with an M.E. degree," it is more specific.

So decide TODAY!

5. Choose a career or educational course you REALLY like.

Yes, just any specific career goal is not enough to make you fly like a rocket towards it.

You must be **passionate** to achieve your career goal. Why? When you are passionate, you will never need a daily push from parents or teachers to attend school everyday, to do homework on time and prepare well before exams.

You will take all the essential steps to succeed in your studies automatically!

Here is some food for thought. In our workshops, we usually ask students what they want to become. Here is what we find again and again…

- Students *who replied instantly* usually scored high in exams.
- Students *who took time* to reply usually scored average marks in exams.
- Students who said, *"I am yet to choose my career"* usually scored below average or had failed the exams.

What is the secret behind that *instant* answer? Students who answered instantly had already chosen the career goal they loved and *had a strong desire to reach it*. This influenced them to study harder!

6. Choose a career that is in *demand*.

Oh dear, it is not enough to choose a career goal that you are passionate about! Your passionate goal should also be *in demand*!

Now how do you cross this hurdle? Here's how…

Ensure that the career you are so passionate about is able to solve some burning problem or fulfils a *basic* need of people. Then you will be in demand.

What is basic and what is not? For example, a career in sports, dance or music does not fulfil a basic need. *This is because most people can survive their entire life without such services!*

But a career that is directly or indirectly connected to providing shelter, food, clothes, education, protection, energy, finance, etc. will be in demand even in times of scarcity. This is because people cannot lead satisfactory lives without these.

Did you say, "*Tendulkar* and *Amitabh Bachchan* are minting crores!"? Great. But what are your chances of being in their place? One in 100 million? But the world needs millions of teachers, managers, engineers and doctors. Why not aim to be the BEST among them? This is much easier!

However, if you still want to act or bat, our best wishes are always with you. Best wishes ONLY!

7. Take the help of others, if required, in choosing a *meaningful* career.

Sometimes, choosing a career goal is not that easy, especially if you have many skills and options. If you face such a situation, seek help from your parents, teachers, seniors, or career counsellor to choose the best career for yourself.

But don't allow others to **impose** their choice on you, especially if you do not like a particular career suggested. Preparing for a career that you dislike is more stressful. Also, you cannot function at full potential in such careers. This is what happened with two of our friends who did not choose the right career…

- One of our friends did MBBS influenced by his parents. But he found it tough and boring. Finally, he changed his career and he is now in the *furniture business*!
- Another friend did B.E. in civil engineering and though he is working as a civil engineer, *he spends more time as a photographer*!

Look around and you will find many mismatches like these. Avoid this. Remember, *when you are in the wrong career, you cannot be the best*.

When you are not at your best, you will not be satisfied and might even earn less, leading to **stress** or other problems. So choose the right career.

8. When you find it difficult to make a choice between two or more career goals, meet people in those careers and collect additional data.

When you have multiple skills and many career options, it is tough to choose a career goal.

The best way to solve this problem is to meet career people from the field you are interested in and seek more information on the sector and future trends. Use this to take the right decision about your career.

At such meetings, ask questions like these and note the answers:

- Will there be enough *demand* for new entrants in this field by the time I finish my education?
- What scope does this have for my *development*?
- What specific *skills* and *qualifications* do I need to enter and succeed here?
- What is the *earning potential*?
- Does it call for *teamwork* or *independent* activity?
- What are the working hours?
- At what *geographic locations* are the openings mostly available?

Answers to these questions will help you take a better decision.

9. Set your academic goals.

Once you have decided on a career goal, plan your steps to reach that goal.

The most important step is to know the percentage of marks or the grade you need to gain *admission* in the course that qualifies you to enter your chosen career.

Now decide the percentage or grade you want in the exams. Be specific. Your brain is designed to hit specific targets.

An example to fix your career and academic goal is given below. For your use, a blank format is given on the next page. Use it to prepare your career goal card. This card also includes two powerful affirmations to repeat daily. Check this card daily and repeat the affirmations several times.

My Career Goal Card

I want to become an *Electronics Engineer*

I want to score *'A' grade* (enter % of marks or grade) in my examination.

Tina

Date: *15-11-2006*   Signature

(Record your career goal on this card and read it DAILY.)

I Want To Become ....

As an Immediate Step to Achieve My Goal, I will Score .... %/Marks/Grade

In .... Exam.

Date: Signature:

Affirmation to Use Daily:

By Regular Study and Frequent Revision
I CAN MASTER Any Subject."

"**I Can Get Whatever** I Want in Life
By Making Efficient Use of My
UNLIMITED Brainpower."

10. Set a subject-wise scoring target.

Most students prepare well for some subjects, but pay less attention to others. The result is tragedy—it's good-bye to their dream career.

Prevent this tragedy by setting specific targets for each subject. Then you will pay equal attention to all subjects in your course.

Check the example below. Use the format on the next page to decide what percentage or grades you want to score in each subject.

Once you complete this, look at it frequently, preferably daily. *Always remember*:

> *You can achieve whatever target you set*
> *by making the right use of your brainpower.*

Sr. No.	Name of Subject	Grade or % of marks obtained in previous exam	Grade or % of marks I wish to score in my next exam
1.	**English**	**68%**	**75%**
Note: Enter your targets in the format given below.			

Sr. No.	Name of Subject	Grades or marks obtained in last exam	Grades or marks I will score in the next exam

Date: Signature

Note: You can modify this format to accommodate your subjects. Make a copy of this page and fill in the blanks. You can use this card as a bookmark, so that you can check it frequently.

11. Choose and record your dream life.

What is this 'dream life'? *Dream life* means to choose and decide exactly what kind of life you want to live in future.

This is very important because your dream life gives a definite purpose to your life. And helps you to live a meaningful and happier life.

How do you choose your dream life? Your dream life will answers questions like:

- What would you like to become when you grow up? *(Your career goal)*
- How much would you like to earn?
- What kind of lifestyle would you like to lead? *(House to live in, things to own)*
- Where do you wish to settle? *(City, country)*
- What kind of life partner do you prefer? *(Imagine the kind of wife/husband you want)*

Answer the above questions carefully. And you will have an idea about your dream life. You will have a picture of how you want to live your life!

Now, now, just don't think about the answers. Or you will soon forget everything. Pull out your notebook or diary. On the top of a page write: *'My Dream Life.'* Then write your answers one by one. Your dream life is ready.

12. Set priorities for your goals.

When you have more than one goal, give top priority to that goal which is very important and which you need to achieve as early as possible. Once you achieve this goal, go to the next one.

For example, if you have written 'My Dream Life', you will certainly get many goals to achieve in life. Now which goal should you achieve first?

Work on the goal that needs immediate attention first. *Give it top priority*. As a student, the most important thing is to prepare for your *career*. And the best way to prepare for this is to study well and score high so that you can gain admission in higher courses easily and do well in job interviews.

This means the immediate goal you should achieve now is—*score higher in the next exam*. This is your top priority. Then come goals like finding a good job, earning money, buying a house, etc.

So start working toward your top priority goal by filling out "*My Career Goal*" and "*My Subject-wise Scoring Targets*" cards, if you haven't done so yet.

13. If necessary, review or change your goals.

You can modify or rewrite your goal completely, if you find a better one. But ensure you don't change your goal frequently.

Changing goals frequently may confuse your brain. As a result, you might lose focus and may not be able to work efficiently to reach your goal.

Change your goal only if the new one will ensure:

- More benefits
- More happiness and satisfaction
- Better future

But be aware that changing your goal drastically or entering a new career field after completing your education, results in *loss of skills and knowledge*.

However, you can minimize this loss by choosing a new career goal in the *same* field to make use of most of your skills and knowledge.

Example: if you don't want to be a practising doctor after completing MBBS, you can become a researcher or teacher in a medical college.

∞

CHAPTER 4

9 Secrets to Fix Goals in Your Mind

1. Generate a strong desire to achieve your goal.

Why generate strong desire? A strong desire helps create a powerful chain reaction of super-success...

Deep, strong desire to achieve a career goal increases your interest in studies. When the interest increases, you automatically learn and remember more. Naturally, your score in the exam shoots up. A high score will help achieve your academic goal. This increases the chance of entering your dream career!

Therefore, almost everything depends on a strong desire to achieve the career goal. So how can you develop a strong, burning desire?

Here's how: breathe your goal, dream your goal, live your goal. Develop a strong desire to enjoy the **fruits** of achieving your career goal. Imagine *vividly* the praises, advantages, and confidence you gain by achieving your goal.

And DECIDE to use ALL the secrets given in this book.

2. Write down your goals.

Writing down goals ensures **enormous** advantages:

- It prevents you forgetting your goal a few days after setting it!
- It makes a stronger impression on your brain. This helps to focus your brainpower on your goal and achieve it more easily.
- It prevents you from spending time and energy on less useful activities.

Therefore, always write down your goals. Where? On cards, notebook, walls of the study room, and even in your computer or any other place you are permitted to write!

Follow suggestions given earlier and use the cards and notebook to write goals and programme your brain to make success *automatic*.

Hey friend, I am not just lecturing you! My life is the result of this super-secret! A notebook I started in 1959 turned me from failure into a first-class student. Another notebook started in 1980 made me a successful parent, engineer, trainer and an author. I also make extensive use of cards.

—*B. K. Narayan*

Secrets given in this book really work. All great people worldwide have used similar ideas to keep their mind focused on the target. Why not you?!

3. Write goals on a stiff card to make it last longer.

You are going to spend many years as a student. So your career, life dream and other cards representing various goals are supposed to last for years. Right?

That's why, it is a smart idea to write down your precious goals on good quality cards.

For best results, use cards of different sizes: to keep in pockets, bag or purse and to display on the walls of your study room or study table!

Remember these points while preparing goal cards:

- If you don't get cards of suitable size in stores, make them yourself.
- Buy few sheets of art paper or drawing/ivory sheets from a stationery store and cut them into various sizes.
- Ivory sheet cards remain bright for a longer period and last longer. And also make you feel proud of your goals!
- You can use cards for different purposes to make your success easy. For example: you can use cards to *focus* your brain on goals, to *master* difficult study topics, to *cultivate* good habits, etc.

4. Write goals in your favourite colour. And you can add pictures too.

Writing down your goal is good. But writing goals in colour and with images is even more powerful.

Such cards appear very attractive and make you look at them again and again. Also, goal cards that are prepared with creativity, colour and images make a *powerful impression on your brain*.

With such goal cards, you can focus your brain on goals more strongly and achieve success with greater ease.

Here are a few useful guidelines to prepare attractive and powerful goal cards:

- ✦ Write on the cards as beautifully as you can, using your favourite colour.
- ✦ Make your cards more powerful by drawing pictures or by pasting colour photos. If required, use a bigger card.
- ✦ If you use photos, choose ones in which you are receiving some prize or certificate. Or use pictures of cars, bungalows or of beautiful places you will visit after realizing your goal.

5. Make at least two copies of each card. Paste one set on the wall or table of your study room. Keep another set in your purse or bag.

Once you prepare your goal cards, it is time to USE them to transform yourself into a super-achiever.

Is it possible to become a super-achiever just with cards? Yes, cards used *effectively* bring about MAJOR changes in you.

What is this effective way? *See your goal cards repeatedly and read your goal with **feelings**.*

For this, we need at least two copies of each card. Here is how to use your various cards:

- ✦ Keep one set of cards in your purse or bag. And display another set on the wall or table in your study room.
- ✦ Read these cards before sudying, before sleeping and after arising in the morning.
- ✦ In the classroom, quickly read the card in your bag or purse to expose your brain to positive messages and to switch on the success-inducing thoughts and habits.

Do not ignore this suggestion. It works. And it takes just 30 seconds.

This little effort can give you the power
to REDESIGN Your Future!

6. LIST all the BENEFITS you would gain by achieving your career goal. And read this list as frequently as possible.

This is the secret weapon of salespersons. Using a list of benefits, they sell their goods and services even to least interested people! You too can benefit in a big way by using this secret.

Why is this so powerful? Everyone likes to live happily and safely. A list of benefits from doing certain things helps us realize that the thing or activity will make us happy and secure.

When we realize this, we develop a strong desire to get that thing done!

Similarly, you can use this secret to develop a strong desire for your career goal and imbed it deeply in your brain. Here is what you must do:

- On a separate page in your dream life notebook list *all the small* and *big benefits* you gain by realizing your career goal. Then read this list frequently.
- Similarly prepare another list of all the small and big benefits *others gain* if you realize your career dream. The 'others' may include your parents, relatives, teachers *et al*.
- Read this list *frequently*. Add more benefits.

7. Use this affirmation daily: *"Yes, I will achieve my goal. I am a born winner."*

The above sentences are simple. Yet they have the power to increase the confidence in yourself and your goal.

While repeating this affirmation: *"Yes, I will achieve my goal. I am a born winner,"* mentally remember all the things achieved so far. Be aware of all the skills and positive qualities you possess.

When you do this for a few weeks, you will feel and act like a born winner. And be able to work toward your career goal more confidently!

By the way: *Do you know what you **really** are?*

Most of us don't! We have put this question to nearly two thousand people of different age groups and positions. We discovered that people do not describe themselves as they really are! Most people *described themselves negatively*. This is the number one cause that makes us underachievers or failures.

Fortunately this can be reversed and you can realize how powerful you really are.

If interested, just use the *free resource* given at the end of this book under *"Source For Additional Help"*.

8. Visualize yourself as having ALREADY achieved your goal.

This is the top secret to achieve great success! And it is very easy to use. Even children can do this.

In this technique, you only have to close your eyes and imagine or visualize what you want. Imagine that you have *already* attained it.

For example, if your career goal is to become an Interior Designer, mentally 'see' yourself already working as an Interior Designer. Imagine yourself planning and decorating rooms of huge bungalows and receiving a big cheque for it! Feel very happy about your success.

This visualization technique makes your success easier. Because visualizing yourself having already achieved your goal ensures these benefits:

- Creates a *"success blueprint"* in your brain by creating a new neuronal network that your brain uses to *guide you* to succeed.
- Increases your belief in yourself. It influences you to think, *"Yes, this is possible. I can achieve it."*
- Motivates you and gives you ideas to work towards your goal.

This visualization technique will be explained in more detail later in this book.

9. Meet people who have already achieved a goal similar to yours.

For example, if your goal is to be a topper in your school or college, meet the previous year's topper. If you want to become a fashion designer, meet the person who is already one.

To benefit from such meetings, ask:

- How did s/he do it? What kind of preparation is required? What books were referred to? Were there any prepared notes or answers for probable questions?
- If tuition is required, who is the best tutor?
- What qualifications and skills are required to enter and succeed in this field?
- Are there any competitive exams? Is guidance available to prepare for such exams? Who is the best tutor for this?

Take notes, and say 'Thanks' when you leave.

∞

CHAPTER 5

6 Secrets to Boost Brainpower

1. The #1 secret of extra brainpower is to USE YOUR BRAIN MORE.

The more you use, the more you get. This is the BIG secret of increasing brainpower.

Brain cells called neurons forming a neuronal network record everything you think and do.

When a *strong* network of neurons is created, you *learn better and remember more.* How do you create a strong network of neurons? *By repetition!*

When you revise information or repeatedly practice some action, a strong network of neurons is automatically created in your brain. So, to learn anything fast and remember better, more practice or revision is required. This book will teach you tricks to make such revisions easier.

In fact, this is like developing muscles. The more you lift weights, the more you develop muscles. If you stop lifting weights, the muscles become weak.

Similarly, *if you stop revising you start forgetting!*

2. Your brain has awesome power to help create whatever you want, *if you USE it*!

The human brain created all the wonderful things you see around yourself, from a simple pencil to a spaceship!

Your brain too can create such wonders, *if you allow it to do so*. So forget ALL "I can't do this" limitations. Have a strong desire to score higher and become a successful student. Have a strong desire to lead a happy and rich life. This allows your brain to expand its power and help you succeed.

Here are some powerful features of your brain:

- ✦ You will *never* be short of brainpower to achieve WHATEVER you want. Your brain is designed to increase capacity on demand. *So demand more to get more.*
- ✦ There are some 20 billion neurons in an adult brain. Most neurons can make up to 20,000 connections with

other neurons. *This capacity to form a huge neuronal network is the **secret** of your unlimited brainpower.* This network *keeps growing* as and when you learn new things! With this network, you will never be short of brainpower.

✦ Research has shown that the human brain can grow and expand even in old age. When aged people learn new things their brain forms new connections! *So keep learning to stay young!*

3. Use emotions to 'switch on' more brainpower and to make learning and remembering easy.

When you do something with **love**, your brain is more stimulated. Your neurons get more excited and interact with thousands of other neurons to help you think and act better.

As a result, mental efficiency and concentration power increases. And you find you can do that work more easily. Not only this, you also have more power to overcome any difficulties that may arise while doing the work you love.

But when you hate what you do, your brain becomes sluggish. Your neurons are less excited and interact less with other neurons. So the work you hate becomes more difficult and you come up with 101 excuses for not doing it!

This is why students with a *strong desire* to score high usually succeed. Their sheer love to succeed stimulates the brain strongly. So such students find studying easier and have better retention powers. What's more, such students can study happily for hours.

But students who hate studying face more problems and end up with poor performances. *It is the emotions at work— **against you or for you!***

4. List all benefits of learning your subjects and love them.

If you want more success in studies, just **love** *your studies!* Your love will stimulate the brain strongly. And you will start learning the topics more easily.

But how do you love your subjects?

The secret: think about ALL the small and big *benefits of learning* every subject and make a list of this.

Think about how each subject helps in your day-to-day life, what they teach you about the world, what knowledge or skills they impart to succeed in your career. Such thoughts will help you find more benefits of studying these subjects.

This list of benefits will give you *reasons* to love your subjects and make you aware of how each subject is important for your success.

Write this list in a diary. Then read it at least once a week. It will increase your interest in studying. *More interest = more brain activity and better learning!*

5. Make changes in your brain and personality to develop success-inducing habits by using two commands: "IGNORE" and "ATTENTION".

Pay *attention* to qualities you want to make stronger and *ignore* those you want to make weaker.

Each time we use a habit, or pay attention to it, it grows stronger in our brain. Attention **activates** the neuronal network on which that habit or quality is already recorded, and the network grows stronger as additional connections are formed. (This is why revision helps in learning.)

Ignoring things does the **opposite**.

If you stop revising lessons, you forget them. If you stop using a bad habit, it gets weaker. This is because ignoring a skill weakens the neuronal network on which it has been recorded.

How do you make practical use of these commands? For example, if you want to get rid of the bad habit of watching TV for long hours, *decide* to 'Ignore' TV and *simultaneously* pay 'Attention' to studies or learning some useful skill. So when the TV serial begins, ignore it and *use this time* to pay attention to studies or another useful activity.

In this way, use these commands to get rid of ALL bad habits that take you away from your goal.

6. To make life and success easier take better care of your brain.

By taking better care of your brain and learning to use its power correctly, you can enjoy many *benefits like*: learning anything fast, scoring high in exams, securing the job you love, being healthy and energetic and so on!

A healthy brain helps you attain these benefits more easily. To keep the brain healthy all your life, follow these steps:

1. Give your brain more of its favourite food, oxygen. It is free! Just take 5-6 deep breaths every hour. Do some physical exercise at least for 30 minutes everyday.

2. Never blame your brain if you don't get the results you want. Instead, keep saying, *"I have a powerful brain," "I can achieve whatever I want by making correct*

use of my unlimited brainpower." Such thinking helps make maximum use of your brainpower.

3. Do mental exercises to keep your brain sharp: solve puzzles or crosswords, read good books, meditate for 15-20 minutes.
4. Eat a balanced diet. Drink at least 8 glasses of water daily. Relax often. Sleep for 8 hours daily.

∞

CHAPTER 6

8 Secrets to Programme Yourself for Success

1. Learn the skills of using "AFFIRMATION" and "VISUALIZATION".

You can get more out of your powerful brain by using mind-controlling skills.

You are ALREADY programmed to think, feel, act and behave in a certain way in various situations. Such programming has been done by your parents, teachers, relatives, peers, and also by exposure to newspapers, TV, etc. All these things are recorded in your brain.

If your present performance is not good, there is every chance that your brain has been fed with many negative programmes!

By using specific affirmation and visualization techniques, you can *replace* negative programmes with powerful, positive, success-building programmes.

In other words, you can "reprogramme" the brain to change your behaviour. *With **repeated** use, this new programme grows stronger and stronger, making success easy for you.*

2. Use AFFIRMATIONS to focus your brain *on what you want*, instead of what you don't want.

In simple words, affirmation is making positive and powerful suggestions *repeatedly*. Affirmation helps programme your brain positively. When you repeat affirmations, they are recorded in your brain strongly and *influence* you to act in a certain way that helps ensure the result you want.

For example, this famous affirmation was created by Emile Coue for his patients: *"Day by day, in every way, I am getting better and better."* When you repeat this affirmation, you give your brain the suggestion to focus on creating good health for you.

Conversely, when you think of health problems, you direct your brain to keep you in *that problem condition*!

So affirmation is a simple yet powerful way to help you focus the brain on what you want!

Affirmation should be *simple, direct* and *positive*. "I am not going to fail in the exam," is incorrect. One of the correct ways is to say, "I will pass my exam with A grades." Another example: "I like to learn Grammar. Grammar helps me speak and write effectively."

You will find more affirmations later in this book to help you achieve greater success in studies.

3. Use affirmations at regular intervals till you get the desired result.

Please keep following things mentally while using affirmations to get lasting results:

- Repeat a chosen suggestion at least 5 to 10 times, twice a day. Remember, the more you repeat, the quicker it will help you. So whenever possible, try to repeat more than 10 times.
- You will see noticeable changes in yourself when you repeat each affirmation about 1000 times, spread over a period of three weeks.
- Affirmations can be said aloud or silently. When you are alone, say them loudly. Say them mentally when there are people around you—in a classroom, playground or with friends.
- Say the affirmation with *feeling*, and *expect* it to work.
- *Don't worry* whether the affirmation will work or not. Just repeat it with interest and enthusiasm. It will work. Worrying only delays or prevents results.
- Be patient and persistent, you will get results. This is a *proven* system.

4. Check your Goal Cards daily till you achieve them and read the contents with great feeling—*then your brain will automatically guide you toward success.*

Your brain has this special property that works wonders for you: when you repeatedly think of any thought or goal with great feelings, it becomes a *dominant thought*. Your brain takes this dominant thought as a target and *influences you automatically* to think and act until that dominant thought becomes a reality.

This is how love affairs begin and why it is *very difficult* to stop them thereafter. The 'love' has become a dominant thought!

Why not use this power to achieve any tough goal? Just LOVE it to achieve it!

Unknowingly I used this power in 1959 to change myself from a *failure to a First-Class student*. I wrote the percentage of marks I wanted to score in my SSLC exam and *saw it daily* till the exam was over. Gradually I began to take more interest in studies, I began to take help to clear my doubts, made frequent revisions and was finally transformed into a First-Class student. I continued to be a First-Class student even in my engineering course—as I continued to set targets!

—*B. K. Narayan*

Amazing, isn't it? If such a simple action can bring about such a big CHANGE in me, imagine what you can do by using ALL the secrets in this book!

5. **Use Visualization to programme yourself to achieve success with enjoyable effort and no stress.**

When you read an interesting storybook do you feel stressed? Do you look at your watch from time to time? No! On the contrary, you will probably get so engrossed in reading the story that you will find it hard to put down.

Reading study books can become as interesting as storybooks when you 'programme yourself' to succeed as a student.

This is the secret behind every top achiever. Top achievers love to score high in their exams. Because of this love, top achievers naturally *daydream about their success*—the best way to programme yourself to succeed as a student.

Now you too can start daydreaming about your academic success by using visualization.

What is visualization? Visualization is a popular mind-programming method. It is similar to daydreaming—just close your eyes and mentally 'see' what you want. Mentally picture yourself achieving your goal successfully!

When you visualize success, it creates a *mental blueprint or plan of what you want* in the brain. The brain uses this blueprint to influence you into taking the *right actions* that lead to success.

6. **To programme yourself effectively visualize your goal with *life-like* details—*using all your senses*.**

Your brain is a biological multimedia super-computer! It records all experiences in many forms—sound, pictures, colour, touch, taste, feelings, movement, balance, and temperature too!

Among these, colourful pictures, sounds or words, movement, touch and *feelings* play a major role in *influencing our behaviour and success.* Feelings or emotions are especially important because they increase the brain's activity during programming or visualization. Increased brain activity means the creation of a strong neuronal network. A strong neuronal network helps you *think and act* automatically in a way that ensures your success.

This is why those who get passionately involved in their goals always succeed. Also, they never feel they are working 'hard' to achieve success because even their work becomes 'enjoyable'!

So the secret of achieving big success in studies **without hard work** is to become passionate about learning various subjects—and of living a **rich** life!

So while programming yourself, imagine your success in detail using all the senses and feelings.

7. **To excel in studies, use the visualization programme given below.**

    1. Sit comfortably on a chair or lie down in bed.
    2. Close your eyes. Take 4-5 deep, slow breaths. As you breathe out, *relax* your body.
    3. *Start creating a series of these wonderful pictures in your mind:* You are sitting at your desk, studying intently. Then imagine yourself sitting in the exam hall, coolly writing answers to all questions. Now imagine the final picture—you are receiving a certificate with the 'A' grade or the percentage you want. You are being hugged by your parents. Teachers and friends are congratulating you.

        Imagine the above pictures as clearly as possible, involving all your senses and *feelings*. Imagine the scenes repeatedly for at least 5 minutes and enjoy it!
    4. Become aware of your surroundings, gently open your eyes, and resume normal activities.

        Repeat the above positive and powerful visualization programme daily, until you notice improvement in your study performance. Do this visualization for 10 to 15 minutes.

8. **Practice visualization before sleeping. The next best time is just after waking up in the morning.**

Visualization just before sleeping makes a deeper impression on the brain. Since it is not interrupted by other activities, your brain has more time to process and retain dreams of success.

Early morning is equally good, since your mind is relatively relaxed. Visualization at this time ensures that whatever you picture now stays 'fresh' in the mind for a longer time.

∞

CHAPTER 7

10 Secrets to Attain 100% Concentration

1. The #1 secret to concentrate 100 per cent on studies is to give TOP PRIORITY to education.

This is one of the unique properties of our brain: *it easily concentrates its energy and power on things that you feel are important*.

Your future depends on the knowledge and skills you acquire as a student. Only *you* will benefit by your education. So decide to give top priority to education. This will automatically draw your mind toward study. Concentration will then become easy.

You can further motivate yourself to give top priority to studies by listing the benefits of education and remembering all those benefits well.

This has been suggested earlier. Please act on that.

+ The most important benefit of good education is it can make *all areas* of your life *rich*: *personal, career, financial, health, love, and spiritual. Always remember this.*

2. Remove external distractions that prevent you concentrating 100 per cent.

Our brain is designed to process all the stimuli that reach our sense organs—sound, light, smell, etc.

This keeps us safe by making us aware of anything that might harm us. So don't blame yourself if you are aware of other things around you and find it hard to concentrate! Instead, remove things that disturb you.

Here is what you can do:

+ *Request* your family to help you study with concentration.
+ Ask them to shut off sources of noise like the TV, radio, etc. during your study hours.
+ If your family wants to enjoy their favourite programme, they can reduce the sound volume.
+ If you are still sensitive to sound, use earplugs or headphones. Of course, without connecting the latter to live music!

- Keep books and other interesting things outside your study room.
- Switch off your mobile phone. And close the door of the study room.

3. Get rid of the biggest enemy of 100 per cent concentration—*internal distractions*!

Internal distractions are things that happen *inside* your brain after closing the doors of your study room, turning off the TV and radio, and putting on your earplugs—your mind starts wandering!

Even though you open your books and stare at them, you find yourself thinking about 101 different things! This is a common problem of all human beings. It is natural for different thoughts to arise in the brain.

How do you solve this problem? Definitely not by fighting them. When you fight any thought, you give it more energy and it gets stronger and more bothersome the next time.

Instead of resisting, simply DECLARE, as below, that you will think only about studies for the next two hours and about other things later!

> "**For the next *2 hours*** (choose a suitable duration) **I will think only about studying *chemistry*...** (or any other subject)."

With repeated use of this self-declaration, you will gradually be able to focus on studies. Initially, your stray thoughts may refuse to go away. Just *ignore* them and keep studying. They will soon stop bothering you for want of energy—your attention!

4. Use the following simple steps to concentrate 100 per cent in classroom or at home, and learn more with less effort:

- Sit comfortably in the chair while studying.
- Take a deep breath every ten minutes.
- Use these questions to involve your brain with the topic at hand: *how, what, when, where, who, why*. That is, *silently* ask questions about the topic while listening to the lecture or reading the study material.

This trick of asking questions while studying keeps you wide awake! This is because your brain has a peculiar characteristic—the moment it hears a question, it goes into search mode till it finds the answer or you ask another question.

Whenever you are questioning and thinking about the topic under study, you are concentrating 100 per cent! Those stray thoughts cannot bother you now.

Also, whatever you study you will understand better. Keep asking the above questions for 3-4 weeks. *It will soon become a habit*. Then you will have the power to concentrate 100 per cent whenever you want.

5. *Recharge your body and mind frequently*: **Before you start studying, and during study breaks, stretch your body. Take 3-4 deep breaths.**

   Understand yourself: Your body-mind system is a huge, complex association of trillions and trillions of living entities—the living cells. They need a constant supply of various nutrients and frequent rest to recharge themselves so that they can work better and serve you efficiently.

   Help your system to serve you better: Nutrients required by your body-mind system are supplied through proper circulation of blood. Whenever you shift from one position to another or reduce the intensity of activity, the cells of your body get time to rest and recharge a bit. This is essential to help you do things smoothly. Otherwise, even simple things can become hard work for you.

   Here is what to do:

   + Stretch like a cat! Stretching relaxes the body, improves blood circulation, and decreases the workload on your brain.
   + Take 3 to 4 slow, deep breaths before and after study sessions to supply oxygen to your brain.
   + While in classroom or at home, sit comfortably without tensing any part of your body.

6. **Use SPECIFIC affirmations to facilitate 100 per cent concentration as long as you want.**

   Yes, you can zoom in to a state of concentration and stay there with the help of specific affirmations.

   By using affirmations you can easily *focus* your brain on study topics as long as you want. This automatically increases concentration power.

   Here are specific affirmations to concentrate better:

   + "I can concentrate *at will*. I love to do *one thing at a time*."
   + "Studies are my top priority. Because studies will help me acquire important skills and knowledge to launch myself into the career I love."

- "For the next *two* hours (or any other duration) I am going to concentrate on studying *physics* (or any other subject). I love *physics*. It is useful and interesting."

Each affirmation triggers positive thoughts that influence you to think and act like a brilliant student! *To make this your habit*, repeat all or any of the affirmations thrice before studies.

7. **Practise giving undivided attention to each activity—even to eating and TV serials!**

   Like any other skill, the skill to concentrate better is cultivated with practise.

   Believe it or not, you already have the power to concentrate 100 per cent. Surprised? What do you think when you are watching a funny TV serial, or a violent fight between the hero and villain, or while reading a good book? *Nothing else!*

   Yes, in the above situations you are so busy concentrating on watching or reading that you don't think about anything else. This is what 100 per cent concentration means. So this proves that you already have the ability to concentrate fully in certain situations.

   Now you just have to transfer this ability to other situations—listening to a lecture in the classroom, studying at home, following a conversation, etc.

   In fact, you can use daily activities as exercises to develop concentration power. Here's an example: when your friend starts talking, mentally say, "I will fully concentrate on what my friend is saying," and then do your best to pay full attention to his words.

8. **Learn to train your mind to stay on ONE activity at any given time:** *on the activity you choose!*

   This is a simple yet powerful method of increasing concentration power. Besides, with this method you can train your mind to do what you want and to concentrate on one activity for a long duration.

   Once you develop this ability, it can become a very useful habit. Can you imagine its power? All the inventions and wonderful things around you came from someone's *focused* mind. You too can have such power by training your mind.

Here are two simple exercises to train your mind to concentrate better:

1. *Hear a particular sound*

Sit quietly and close your eyes. Imagine you are hearing the sound of a violin, flute or any other musical instrument. Choose *only one* instrument *at a time*. Imagine that sound for two minutes. Now choose another instrument.

2. *Do mental mathematics*

Close your eyes and start multiplying numbers in your mind. Start with two digits, then move on to more digits.

9. NEVER say you can't concentrate—this reinforces your *inability* to concentrate. Instead, say, "I CAN concentrate on anything for any length of time."

Repeated thoughts and actions become habits.

Most of us have repeatedly entertained some of these negative thoughts:

- "I can't concentrate fully."
- "It is impossible to concentrate 100 per cent."
- "It requires years of practise to learn to concentrate fully even for a minute."

Repetition of such thoughts has created a belief that concentration is tough.

If you have done the exercises given on the previous pages, you already know that every time you *practise* your ability to concentrate improves.

Here is another trick for faster improvement in concentration: whenever you feel you are concentrating better, immediately *reinforce* it with these affirmations:

- "My concentration is improving."
- "Day by day I am able to concentrate longer and better."

10. It helps to concentrate better if you cultivate the habit of *studying as per your timetable*.

When you study as per a timetable you feel good and calm. You are hopeful about finishing all the course material before the examination.

Believe it or not, this feeling of calmness helps you concentrate better while studying because there is no tension about how you will manage to study everything.

Make it a policy to study as per your timetable. You may already be using some kind of timetable. If not, you will learn more on how to prepare an effective study timetable in the next chapter.

Once you prepare your timetable, use it regularly to gain all these benefits:

- Concentrate better while studying
- Make your student life stress-free
- Devote enough time to cultivate all the essential skills you need to live better.

It is worth your weight in gold to cultivate this habit. The next chapter will teach you know how to prepare and use the study timetable effectively.

∞

CHAPTER 8

9 Secrets to Manage Your Time Efficiently

1. Prepare a monthly timetable and allot enough time to fully master all subjects before the exam.

Remember, *the things you measure you achieve*. A monthly timetable helps you prepare properly and avoid the fear of failure.

The best way to prepare a monthly timetable is to use a calendar. Hang a calendar in your room and mark the study topics you want to cover in a month. Use a calendar that has enough space to write the names of your subjects.

If you don't get such calendar, prepare your own one with plain paper.

Also mark dates of homework submission, practical submission and dates of tests and exams, etc. on the same calendar. Done? Now your monthly timetable is ready.

Start studying according to this timetable. You will not waste time. This method works best because a calendar has more visual impact. It easily attracts attention and you will be able to track activities properly.

2. Prepare a weekly timetable.

The next step is to prepare a weekly timetable. Don't worry. This is also easy to prepare.

In the weekly timetable, include all the *main activities* that you have to do in a week. Write how many lessons or other study work you have to complete in a week.

For example, you can write:

In this week I have to…

- learn two lessons of geography,
- solve ten maths problems,
- finish a practical report on the last science experiment,
- prepare for next week's English test,
- draw a diagram of the brain, etc.

Just quickly write down a short list of all the main study activities you have to do in a week. Your weekly timetable is ready! It's that simple.

You can write your weekly timetable in a separate diary or notebook. Or you can also mark it on the calendar, if space permits, in short words. Choose the one you like.

3. Finally, prepare a daily timetable.

Now we come to the most detailed timetable. *This is the most important timetable*. It helps you plan each hour of your time properly and use it efficiently.

In the daily timetable, list activities on hourly basis. Starting from the time you wake up, write what you will do during each hour of the day. Note how many lessons or work you will finish in a day, and at what time.

You can prepare your daily timetable in the form of a quick list. Just write what you have to do in a day in short words. Ensure you write about each activity, one below the other, as it will be easy to read.

You can't use a calendar for this timetable. Also, don't write your daily timetable on a loose sheet of paper that can get misplaced.

The best thing to do is to write it in a small dairy or notebook. Now keep this where it is easily noticeable.

4. Maintain a detailed diary of activities and get more time to achieve your goal.

This is a great technique to find out where your time is wasted. For this, just record all your activities for the next three days. Again, use a diary or a notebook. Record how you spend your time, each day, for the next three days.

Write this in as much detail as possible. For example, you can write what you did every hour or half hour each day.

At the end of three days, check activities that are not helping you, directly or indirectly, in achieving your goal.

Avoid such time-wasting activities.

If you are not an exception, you will be shocked to know that about 50 per cent of your wakeful time is spent on unimportant activities.

Remember:

"Amount of study time = Amount of information learnt"

So give more time to study
Use your time well

5. Avoid habitual time-wasting friends tactfully or even better, use them to study more.

How do you get rid of a common problem: *time-wasting friends?*

Everyone is not as motivated as you to excel in studies. You may have one or more of such 'less motivated' students as friends.

When they are bored, they may visit you and unknowingly end up wasting your time too. How do you handle such friends? You can't tell them point-blank that they are wasting your time and hurt their feelings. At the same time, you don't want to lose your study time. To handle this delicate situation, use two tricks:

- After speaking with your friend for a minute or two, tactfully ask him or her to join you in studies! Ask your friend to explain some subject or repeatedly pester your friend with questions about studies.
- If your friend is strong in some subjects, get your doubts cleared in that subject.

Either your friend will answer your questions and help you or run away! The chances of that friend coming to your house again whenever s/he feels bored will then be very slim!

6. Do your homework the same day.

Believe it or not, this is a real time-saver.

Can you eat the entire day's food in one go?

Can you drink all the water of one day in a single gulp? You would choke. This is what happens to students who sleep for many days and wake up when the exam is close. Then they complain they did not get enough time!

But lack of time is not the only problem caused by such behaviour. These students develop another habit that is the biggest enemy of success—procrastination or putting off things until the last moment or not doing things on time.

Many have this bad habit throughout life and end up achieving low success in their career or business.

So RESOLVE to do all your assignments on time. Finish your homework the same day. Study daily.

The *golden habit* of doing work on time will benefit you throughout life.

7. Use campus time to study more.

Whenever there is an off period, don't waste time. Remember, acquiring knowledge and skills is your MAIN BUSINESS as a student. *The quality of your student life will directly influence the quality of your future.*

There are many benefits when you focus on playing your student role better: learning will become easy, exams will not seem stressful, and you will acquire higher educational degrees easily. Your success will be INSURED!

So here are some ways to make best use of campus time:

- After class, stretch in your chair and take a few deep breaths. Then go to the library or a place where you will not be disturbed, and complete some homework.
- Discuss the day's teaching with your friends. This serves as a good revision.
- Discuss things happening in the field of your dream career.

8. If you commute by bus or train, use that time to mentally revise the day's lecture.

This is a neat trick to get more time. Use the commute time for revision! You will not only make efficient use of time, but also remember more.

Here are tips to help you with mental revision while commuting:

- Find a place in the bus or train where you can sit properly.
- If this is not possible, stand as comfortably as you can.
- Now, mentally revise what you studied today in class. Don't allow your thoughts to wander aimlessly. Do this until your bus stop or station comes.
- You can do this revision easily if you mentally ask questions like: "What did I study today? What were the important topics?" Then recall those topics. By asking questions, you will remember everything you studied.
- If you have a Walkman or Mp3 player, record your notes and listen to them while commuting.

9. **Always study as per the timetable. Whenever you do this, praise yourself. Give yourself a special treat!**

We need as much encouragement as possible to do good things! Whenever you follow the timetable faithfully, praise yourself: "I am great. I am smart. I am following my study timetable properly."

This will *strengthen* the success habit. Each time, you will be able to follow the study timetable more easily!

The habit of following your own rules and plans will pay enormously ALL your life. Master this habit!

Besides self-praise, reward yourself with a simple treat like eating your favourite food or watching a movie you like or reading a good book, etc. This will make you happy and encourage you to follow your timetable regularly.

∞

CHAPTER 9

8 Secrets to Become More Energetic

1. Inculcate a strong desire to be healthy and energetic and follow health rules.

Being healthy and energetic helps you in becoming a top student. When you are healthy and energetic, your brain functions at optimum level easily. Your body can work longer hours.

Therefore, have a strong desire to be healthy and fit. This desire will *motivate you* to take good care of your health. It will ensure enthusiasm to follow good health rules like:

- Exercising regularly
- Eating a balanced diet
- Drinking sufficient water, etc.

You will learn more about health rules in this chapter to help you avoid dangerous factors that create health problems: junk foods, wrong eating habits, unhealthy thoughts and emotions.

2. Drink at least eight glasses of water a day.

Our body is 70 per cent water. If you don't drink sufficient quantities of water, many body functions will be adversely affected.

Shortage of water badly affects:

- Proper digestion and absorption of food
- Blood circulation
- Elimination of waste from the body

In fact, prolonged shortage of water causes greater health problems and disease. But you can avoid all these easily.

Just drink at least eight glasses of filtered water daily. Have more during extended physical activity and summer.

Do remember—you *cannot* make up shortage of water by consuming soft drinks, coffee, tea and other beverages. These drinks have diuretic properties and make your body lose more water! Just drink plain water. It will keep you healthier.

3. Exercise your mind and body everyday to stay healthy and energetic.

Exercise is the best way to keep your mind and body fit, healthy and energetic.

You can keep your body fit by regularly doing any of the following popular exercises:
- Brisk walking
- Jogging
- Yoga
- Sports-related exercises like swimming, cycling, weightlifting, etc.

Just physical exercise is not enough, though. Your brain also needs exercise.

Here are some simple activities to stimulate the brain:
- Reading motivational books
- Narrating and listening to stories
- Painting
- Chess
- Solving puzzles

These activities fire your imagination, increase the neuronal network in your brain and keep you mentally fit and alert.

4. Sleep 8 hours daily to be healthy and energetic.

Sleep and rest play a vital role in keeping you fit and making you a successful student. Your brain is very sensitive to the lack of sleep and rest. During sleep, a part of your brain is busy in regeneration of your whole system. The brain also stores what you learn during your wakeful hours.

Students who do not get sufficient sleep have memory problems and poor learning abilities. Research also indicates that lack of sleep increases the risk of diabetes, high blood pressure, etc.

Therefore, do not study more by reducing the sleep or rest period. Sleep for at least 8 hours daily. This rule also applies during exams! Most students stay awake the entire night or sleep only 3-4 hours. This is harmful and can decrease mental efficiency and memory power.

Good sleep is important for success in studies. To sleep well and ensure good rest, use this trick: when you lie down in bed, stretch slowly, take a few deep breaths, breathe normally and keep the mind focused on the rhythm of breathing till you fall asleep.

5. Cultivate a positive mental attitude to be healthy and energetic.

Your mental state affects your body chemistry.

When you are happy, cheerful and optimistic your body chemistry too changes to a state that keeps you healthy and energetic.

The opposite is also true! Negative thoughts, hatred, jealousy, fear, and pessimism adversely affect your body chemistry. And you feel depressed, angry, or tense. This state is not good for your health.

Positive feelings and thoughts are very important to maintain good health and stay energetic. So cultivate a new habit—*being cheerful and positive every moment of your life.* When cheerfulness is a habit, all things are easy for you.

From now onwards, decide to feel good, act good and expect to be healthy everyday. To develop a positive attitude, repeat this affirmation thrice daily:

"Day by day, in every way, I am getting better and better and better."

6. Avoid people who are critical, irritable, and habitually negative.

Some people habitually see the negative side in everything—parents, teachers, relatives, the school and everything that touches their life. They always find fault and complain bitterly.

Due to this negative tendency they are rarely happy. The best way to deal with such people is to avoid them as far as possible. In their company, you will only see darkness and soon find fault with everything!

Move away from darkness. Stay with light. Make friendship with positive people. Then you will not fall into the trap of negative thinking.

But if you are in a situation where you cannot avoid negative people, follow this:

- Do not react to their negative behaviour. Be calm. Tell yourself: it is *their* problem.
- Ask questions that make them see the positive side of things.
- Regularly read motivational books.

7. When life seems dull and boring, check your list of goodies.

The list of goodies is nothing but a list of success, sweet memories, and the good things in your life. It is a very good antidote for depression, anxiety and other problems. So prepare one and keep it handy.

To prepare a list of goodies, check your list of successes, goals and dreams. Then add to these better things in your diary. List all the advantages you have today, which many don't:

- ✦ Fit body and good health
- ✦ Good food, good home, good clothes
- ✦ Caring parents, good school, good friends
- ✦ A country with freedom and democracy

The above list has just some examples of the wonderful things you have today. Most of us do not appreciate these things until we lose them. So be aware of these and celebrate life. Be grateful to God or nature that has granted all these goodies to you.

8. Programme yourself to be healthy and energetic all life. There is no need to be sick and weak!

Use this simple mind programming exercise before sleeping. This powerful suggestion regenerates your body and mind to be healthy, energetic and youthful:

- ✦ "Now I am going to sleep. During sleep, my body and mind will be refreshed and regenerated to keep me young, healthy, and energetic. When I wake up in the morning, I will feel fresh and energetic."
- ✦ Repeat thrice or till you fall asleep.
- ✦ When you wake up in the morning, smile with happiness for being alive, healthy and energetic. Say, *"I expect only good things and good people to come into my life."*

Do this daily. You will enjoy life more.

∞

CHAPTER 10

10 Secrets to be on Good Terms with Your Teacher!

1. Arrive in the classroom before the teacher does.

First, be clear on *why* to be on good terms with teachers. When you maintain good relationships with teachers, *you get many advantages*: a teacher's attention on your progress, the willingness to help you solve your problems, encouragement to help you excel in studies.

Also be aware of the drawbacks if you are not on good terms with teachers: you will hate their classes, or won't fully concentrate on what they teach. All this will affect your learning and marks in exam. In fact, even their subjects might be hard to master!

So never hurt your relationship with teachers. But *this does not mean* you do special or undesirable things to gain their favour. Just be a *good student*. Follow the secrets given in this chapter.

The first secret is: be in the classroom before your teacher enters!

2. Sit in front, if possible. Or sit where you can maintain eye contact with the teacher.

This is a simple way to be on good terms with the teacher. Every teacher knows that only those students *interested* in studies prefer to sit in the front row. So the teacher will automatically perceive you as a good student.

Also, sitting in front has many benefits:

- Less distractions.
- Clear visibility of the blackboard.
- You can hear the teacher better.
- Better concentration and learning in the classroom itself.

All these are big advantages that make success easier! Most students who excel in studies choose to sit in front. Be one of them.

Do not worry about the disadvantage—facing most questions from your teacher! If you can't answer some questions, it is not a shameful thing. But sitting in the back due to this fear is shameful. Besides, fear of the teacher's questions can work in your favour—you will study better and learn more.

So sit in front, and enjoy all the benefits.

3. Pay total attention. Listen when the teacher explains.

Teachers love students who pay attention and listen to what they are teaching. So when your teacher teaches, listen carefully. Also ensure your teacher *knows* you are paying attention!

Here are some tricks to ensure your teacher knows you are paying attention and also to help improve your concentration in class:

- Look at your teacher frequently when s/he is teaching. But ensure you don't stare blankly at the teacher. S/he will know immediately that you are physically present but mentally absent.
- Nod your head intermittently to show you are listening.
- Don't stare out of the window repeatedly.
- Don't yawn or look bored.

So pay attention and profit immensely.

4. *Be eager to answer questions.*

Teachers love students who answer questions. It shows the student is paying attention in class, studying properly, understanding clearly and wants to succeed. So always answer questions promptly. You can answer easily if you revise lessons at home.

However, many students dislike answering in class because they fear making mistakes. They also fear classmates might make fun of them if they answer incorrectly.

When you hate to answer or are afraid, your brain cannot provide the answer even if you know it! Emotions like fear prevent you from recalling answers quickly. So give up fear. It will hinder your success. Instead, be confident that you can answer any question.

Also use this trick to remember answers quickly: when the teacher asks a question, remember any word or picture *related* to the answer. This will help you recall the entire answer easily.

5. If you don't understand anything, ask questions. Do not be shy!

This secret also helps you be on good terms with teachers! When you ask your teacher to explain something you don't understand, it shows you are *interested* in learning.

So if you don't understand anything, ask the teacher to explain it. Don't be shy.

Ask yourself frequently: *Why I am in the classroom?* The answer is clear: *to learn skills and acquire knowledge to live a better life.* You are spending a lot of money and time for this. So it is your *right* to know things fully.

But be aware of two points before asking questions:

- If a teacher has a policy of answering questions at the end of the class, don't ask beforehand. Also, some teachers don't like to answer questions during the class. If so, ask them after the class is over.
- Never ask questions to test the knowledge of your teacher! Teachers can easily sense this and might get angry with you. So beware!

6. Be *genuinely* interested in what teachers teach.

Yes. Have *real* interest in what a teacher is teaching in class. Genuine interest helps you absorb everything like a sponge. Also, with this you will find it easier to do beneficial things in class:

- You will pay attention effortlessly
- You will listen properly
- You will sit calmly
- You will learn quickly

There's another benefit: when you are interested in a particular topic, your face automatically indicates interest. Consequently, your eyes will be alive with enthusiasm and curiosity and you will not stare at your teacher *blankly*! This shows your teacher you are *listening* to everything in class. Such students are the teacher's favourite.

So be interested in what is being taught. You can feel such interest easily if you love ALL your subjects. As explained earlier, you can develop such love *by thinking about the subjects' benefits.*

7. **Take notes in class. This is an easy way to show you are a good student.**

When the teacher begins to teach, take notes. This simple act will show your teacher...
- You are alert
- You are listening
- You are interested in learning

The teacher will naturally remember you as a sincere student!

Of course, there are other advantages of taking notes in class. For example, you will not forget the things taught in class when you reach home.

In the pages ahead, there is a separate chapter explaining how to take notes in class.

But remember one point: some teachers *do not* like students writing in class. You might have also come across teachers who say, "Don't write while I am speaking. Look at me, listen and understand first. Write notes later."

If you encounter such teachers, do as they say. But do write down key points after the class!

8. **Attend class regularly. This is another way to make your teacher happy.**

Students who loves studies attend class regularly. So the best way to impress your teacher is to attend classes regularly. Every teacher likes such students.

Besides, for each class you pay in terms of money and time. If you miss a class, you lose a lot.

First, you lose that day's lessons. The second loss is bigger—failing in your duty as a student. This habit of not attending to one's duties will affect your success now and in future. *So make it a policy to attend every class.*

There is another advantage in deciding to attend all classes: *you will not fall sick!* Yes, when you are *eager* to attend all classes your brain helps you remain healthy and fit throughout the year.

Of course, there may be times when you cannot attend class due to unavoidable situations. Then don't worry. Go ahead and miss it!

9. **Complete ALL assignments on time. It's the fastest way to establish good relations with the teacher.**

Whenever you are given homework or project work, complete it properly and submit it on time. This is the best way to impress a teacher and the quickest way to make a teacher say, "You are good." Teachers know only committed students complete all their assignments on time.

What's more, this habit will also help you achieve faster progress in your career and life. Being punctual, finishing work on time, and keeping all your promises are highly valued. Since this is *rare, people with this habit are preferred everywhere.*

10. **Don't overdo things. Don't try to impress too much; this may backfire!**

A timely warning: don't try to impress teachers too much to be on good terms. Don't go overboard.

Teachers don't like it. Just be an honest and sincere student. Then teachers will automatically like you.

This rule applies in all areas of life …

>   ***Don't overdo things to impress others.***

Just do your work as best you can. Others will automatically respect you.

∞

CHAPTER 11

12 Secrets to Learn More in Class

1. **Don't go to class on an empty stomach; your brain will not like it! Have a good breakfast.**

    Attending class means lot of work for your brain, which has to understand, analyse, and record the information you are learning and store it for future use.

    To do all this work *efficiently*, your brain needs enough supply of *nutrients, oxygen and water*. Ensure you supply these in generous quantities.

    Else you will face many problems like:
    - Lack of concentration
    - Low neuronal activity in the brain resulting in weak registration of topics
    - Poor learning
    - More study at home!

    It is easy to prevent these problems: eat a good breakfast, drink enough water and take a few deep breaths.

2. **Before leaving home be in positive mode and enter the class with abundant energy and desire to learn.**

    Do the following; it takes just a couple of minutes. With practice, you reach this state in a few seconds.
    - Sit comfortably in a chair.
    - Close your eyes, take four to five deep breaths. While exhaling, relax the body.
    - Visualize yourself commuting happily, safely, and entering school or college with a smile on your face. As you enter the school or college premises, say silently, *"I love my school/college, I like my teachers, and I love to learn all subjects, I am so eager to attend class."*
    - Open your eyes. Get up slowly and go to school or college with a smile on your face.

    When you enter the school/college premises, repeat the above suggestion mentally.

This orientation exercise helps you *start your day with enthusiasm and to learn more in class.* This is the secret of achieving more with less effort.

Do this daily till it becomes a habit.

3. Arrive in class before it begins. You won't miss anything.

A successful student likes to save time and learn more with less effort. Arriving in class before it begins is one of the best ways to save time. You will not miss any information and not have to waste your lunch or break time asking friends what was taught in class.

Also, always remember: *you are investing* **15 to 20 years** *of your life, a lot of your parents' money, and sheer efforts to get yourself educated.*

It is up to *you* to gain maximum returns from this HUGE investment. So get all the benefits you can.

If you always keep this attitude in mind, you will automatically do more right things. You will also *practise* all the secrets presented in this book.

4. Sit where you can hear and see properly. If possible, sit in front.

This is a time-tested secret to learn more in class.

Whenever you get the chance, sit in the front row in class. You will then get many benefits, such as:

- You can see the teacher and blackboard better
- You can hear better
- You can concentrate better

You can easily get a place in the front row if you come early to class.

What if every student's seat in class is fixed and you find yourself sitting at the back daily?

In such cases, simply increase your focus. Sit comfortably in your chair, take a deep breath and keep your eyes glued to the teacher. Follow every word. Then you will be able to concentrate more easily and your mind will not wander.

But if you have a vision problem and can't see or hear properly in the back, request your teacher to change your seating arrangement.

5. Before the teacher comes, do a quick revision of the previous lecture.

This is the biggest secret of learning anything really FAST. When you do this quick revision, you are using a proven memory doctrine that helps you remember and recall things easily: the principle of ASSOCIATION.

Here's how it works: when you revise the previous day's lecture, you refresh the information stored in your brain. Now, when your teacher teaches today, your brain *associates or links* today's information with the information already stored. This helps in strong recording of information in your brain. As a result, you understand easily and *remember more*.

So a quick revision is the best way to remember more and learn fast in class. You can do this quick revision by glancing through the previous notes.

But what if your teacher starts a new lesson? Then, if you have the textbook with you, quickly browse through the new lesson by scanning the headlines, sub-headlines and sketches. When you do this, an outline of the new lesson you will learn is recorded in your brain and helps you learn better and faster!

6. Love and respect institutions and teachers.

Do you like all your teachers? Do you like your school or college? If you answer 'yes', you are both intelligent and lucky.

Liking your teachers and school ensures one big advantage: you will be able to concentrate *totally* in every class.

If you answer 'no' or like some teachers but dislike others, you are in trouble. Because...

Your attitude, your thoughts, your feelings
affect your academic success!

If you dislike your teachers or school, you will not learn much due to a strange trait of your brain:

- Love leads to higher brain activity, resulting in better learning.
- Hate leads to low brain activity in recording lessons, resulting in less learning.

So start liking your teachers, school or college, *unconditionally*.

You will become a more successful student, *easily*.

7. Concentrate fully on the lesson/lecture.	**W**ith the following steps you can concentrate fully and learn better:

- Sit comfortably in your chair. This improves blood circulation and increases alertness.
- Take a few slow, deep breaths to calm your mind and remove distracting thoughts.
- Then tell yourself mentally, "*Now I will concentrate fully on the lecture. I like to learn history* (or the topic you are about to learn)."
- Now pay attention to your teacher's lecture. When your teacher explains, *silently* keep asking questions like: *how, what, when, where, who,* and *why*. As explained earlier, when you are in question mode, other thoughts cannot enter the mind and disturb concentration.

When you do the above, you automatically prepare both your mind and body to concentrate more and learn better.

8. Take proper notes to remember what you learn and revise later.	**D**on't forget this secret! Writing notes in class is the only way to remember, weeks later, what happened!

Besides, taking notes helps you in three more ways:

- You concentrate better.
- You get important points 'readymade'; with this you can prepare detailed notes at home.
- You can use class notes for revision.

In the next chapter, you will learn effective ways of taking notes.

9. After the lecture is over, quickly revise it by going through your notes.	**T**his is a 'micro-revision.' It takes only a minute or so, but is powerful enough to *stop* you from forgetting what you just learnt in class.

How does it work? Your brain records whatever you learn by forming a neuronal network. And the brain continues strengthening or *consolidating* your new learning for some time, even after you stop learning. If you help the brain *complete* this process, you will recall your new learning better.

Micro-revision is the best way to help your brain in this process.

So after your teacher leaves the class, immediately revise what you learned by quickly reading the main points in your notes.

10. **Before the next class begins, stretch and relax your body. Take a few deep breaths. Drink a glass of water, if required.**

Your brain is a biological supercomputer. It requires an adequate supply of many nutrients to help you learn and work efficiently. Frequent relaxation, deep breathing, and drinking water recharges your brain, providing it with more oxygenated blood.

Do this before the start of every class and you will concentrate better and learn more in class.

You can also use this trick at home or before any activity. You can do this before leaving for school. This will help you stay more alert on the road, avoid accidents and reach your destination safely.

11. **Bring your concentration back to focus before the next class begins by using suggestions given earlier in this chapter.**

Most students don't concentrate fully in class. As a result they learn very little in class and subject themselves to 'overwork' at home.

This can be avoided by concentrating fully in every class and finishing your learning in class itself.

In secret #7 of this chapter, we have explained a simple strategy to concentrate fully in class. Use this. It only takes a few seconds.

12. **At home, recall and outline the contents of the day's lessons.**

This is one of the *best* secrets to prevent memory problems and learn more with less effort. If you don't do this, you will forget about 80 per cent of what you learnt in class within 24 hours.

But by remembering and outlining (writing detailed notes of what you learnt) *on the same day*, you can prevent this loss.

When you use the ideas given in this chapter *together*, your success in studies will become child's play.

So *put them into **REPEATED** use till they become a habit.*

∞

CHAPTER 12

10 Secrets to Take Better Notes In Class

1. **Write the names of topics at the top centre of the page. Write the date and name of the teacher on the top or left side.**

   We know you have heard this before. But it is worth mentioning. Because only by following a proper system will you be able to take important notes in class that will ensure effective revision at home.

   So follow the basics. Always write notes by first writing the name of the lesson or topic in the centre, then writing the date and name of your teacher either on the top left or right side of the page.

2. **Allocate different parts of the page for noting different information to make notes more useful.**

   Here's how to do this:
   - Vertically fold the page and roughly divide it into a larger left and smaller right half.
   - Write notes on the left half.
   - On the right side, write other details like: examples, references, questions, doubts, etc.

   In this way, you will have more information at a glance on each page. This will help you read notes easily and quickly.

3. **To make notes really useful note down as much as possible of:** *key points, key words, sketches, figures, formulae* **and** *probable questions* **on the topic being taught.**

   If you write important points about the topic, it will be very useful afterwards.

   By reading such important points you can:
   - Understand easily
   - Revise properly
   - Remember better
   - Prepare well for the exams

   So listen attentively and note all important points.

   The important points you should write:
   - Definition, laws or formulae.

- ✦ Important word or description about a particular topic or object.
- ✦ Function or significance of particular topic or object.
- ✦ Sketches or tables. If your teacher draws any figure, copy it quickly.

So be an *active* listener in class and note important points in your notebook. However, if your teacher dictates notes in class, you don't have to worry about anything! Just write it all quickly.

4. Leave a few blank lines at the end of each page to add any extra information later.

While reading your notes at home, you might recall some related information, key words, examples or questions.

Or you might get some ideas or better answers to some questions asked by your teacher.

To write down this new information, you need more space. So it is a good idea to leave some blank lines at the end of every page. This is a smart way to create good notes to help you with better revision.

5. Pay attention to what the teacher says is 'important'. Mark that topic or information.

On each topic, many questions can be asked. And each subject has many such topics. So the number of probable questions in an exam is huge! This makes it hard to guess what questions will be asked.

Teachers are aware of this difficulty. So to make things easier for students, they usually stress some questions or topics as important.

Especially be alert when the teacher says:

"This point is important."

"This question can be asked on the topic."

Note such points, otherwise you will forget this. You can use a red pen to mark these topics. Such topics usually appear in the examination or are later useful in your career.

6. Note the questions asked in class. They might also be asked in the exam.

This is one of the short-cut secrets to success. Besides important points, write all questions asked by your teacher in class.

These questions help you in two ways:
- ✦ The same questions or similar ones might be asked in the exams.

- These questions serve as model questions for practice and revision.

At home, find *proper* answers to all such questions.

Note these answers in your notebook. This will not only help you revise lessons properly but also help you gain writing practice for the exam.

7. **Maintain friendship with those who take good notes in class.**

    You need such friends. Sometimes you may miss class, or your teacher might explain some topics faster, and you may not be able to note all points.

    In such situations, you need friends who are good students like you, so that you can copy their notes.

    So cultivate friendship with better students. Here's a tip for this: help them first. If they need anything, help them get it. Also, try to sit with them in class.

8. **If necessary, ask your teacher or friendly seniors how to take notes.**

    In this chapter and the next, you will find secrets to take good and effective notes. Use all these.

    Also ask friendly seniors or your teacher if they know a better way to take notes. You may pick up some valuable tips.

    If possible, use digital MP3 voice recorders for complex topics. If you sit in the front row, you can record what your teacher is saying even if you keep the device in your purse or pocket. At home, listen to this recording and make notes.

9. **Read class notes on the same day and, if possible, within one to two hours.**

    It is important to read notes as early as possible, after the class is over. So read notes on the *same day* they are made.

    If possible read your notes quickly *at the end of that period*. This is the best time for the first revision.

    The next best time is when you return home. *But never postpone it to the next day.*

    Immediate revision prevents forgetting things you learnt. It *reinforces* what you learnt in class and helps the brain strengthen the neuronal network that has recorded the information.

    Immediate revision has another benefit: you will be able to recall any point that you might have missed earlier while your teacher was teaching. Now you can write down those missed points easily in your notes.

10. Mark points you did not understand in your class notes.

While reading the notes, if you don't understand any point, mark it in pencil. Then do any of these three to clear your doubts:

- Ask your friend to clarify such points
- Ask your teacher to clear your doubt
- Refer to related books on the subject

Use the above techniques to get doubts cleared quickly, preferably on the same day.

Do not accumulate doubts. Else, you may not understand things taught in the next class. You may also not be able to answer correctly if your teacher asks any related question.

So do not hesitate to take the help of friends or teachers to get doubts cleared. This helps you be in the list of successful students. *Unsuccessful students live with doubts.* They are ashamed of asking others.

So give up your shyness. Seek help and you will receive it.

∞

CHAPTER 13

13 Secrets to Take Detailed Notes

1. **Make notes in your own words.**

    In college, class notes are not enough to study for exams. You need to make more detailed notes at home. While preparing such notes, use your own words. This has many benefits. It:

    + Builds your expression power
    + Increases your word power
    + Ensures *unique* answers in your own words
    + Helps you read and learn quickly
    + Helps you remember more

    Even if it is not easy for you to make notes in your own words due to **lack of word power**, we suggest you *keep trying*. The advantage of writing notes in your own words is too immense to ignore.

    Also, read the chapter '6 Secrets to Read Faster and Understand Better' to improve your word power so that you can write notes easily.

2. *To prepare thorough and effective notes*, **refer to class notes, textbooks and other books suggested by your teacher, and** *think creatively*—**especially on the practical use of** *that* **information.**

    This is the best secret to prepare good notes that make studying easier.

    As said earlier, refer to everything you can—class notes, textbooks and books suggested by the teacher. Then think creatively: which information is more important, which point explains the topic better, which table or diagram should you use... Then start writing your notes.

    By studying, analysing and thinking creatively, you will not only be able to prepare thorough notes, but also be able to prepare *better answers* to questions that may be asked in the exams.

    Furthermore, you will get a powerful advantage by doing all the above...

    *You will become an **active** learner.*

Blindly copying words from books is not enough. You have to exercise your creative learning. You have to *think deeply* about the question and the probable answers. Then choose the best answer. This is called active learning. *This learning makes higher education easy for you.*

3. To prepare effective notes and model answers, first write a brief outline.

How do you start writing your notes?

Begin by writing a short outline—important points or headlines and sub-headlines one below the other. Writing an outline initially has many advantages:

- An outline helps to choose the right points, key words, and information on the topic
- It helps to write detailed notes easily
- It is especially useful when you have to write essays or lengthy answers

Writing an outline has another big benefit: the next time you open your notes you will have an instant idea of the topic by just glancing at the outline.

What's more, you can do a *quick revision* of your notes by reading the main points in the outline. When you read the main points your brain refreshes the entire topic automatically.

4. Stick to an outline while writing details. Elaborate each point using the outline.

After you prepare an outline, explain each point or keyword in detail. For example, suppose you are preparing notes on the heart. First write a short outline using a headline and sub-headline like this:

Heart
    Position
    Structure
    Diagram
    Function
    Importance
    Taking care

Now write in detail by explaining each point in the outline. That's all.

While writing essays or lengthy answers, elaborate each key idea or point included in the outline in a *separate paragraph*.

Use examples, tables, diagrams, and references wherever required.

5. **Whenever possible, write notes point-wise.**	**N**otes written in lengthy paragraphs appear 'heavy to read.' Just looking at lengthy paragraphs makes you feel bored and discourages frequent revisions! But notes written point-wise appear 'light' and *invite* you to read! You can make notes more attractive by using: ✦ Symbols ✦ Bullet lists (just as we have done here!)
6. **If it is not possible to write in points, write notes in short paragraphs of 3-4 lines.**	**I**t may not be possible always to write notes in points or bullet lists. Then write notes using short paragraphs of 3 or 4 lines. Use long paragraphs only if absolutely necessary. You can write in short paragraphs easily if you restrict a paragraph to *one idea*, keyword or main point. After giving details of that particular point, make a new paragraph. In this way, you can prepare good notes that will be easy to read, understand and remember. Remember, examiners find it hard to check answers written in long paragraphs. Then there is a risk that you may not get full marks, even if you have written the complete answer.
7. **Make notes easily readable with short sentences.**	**I**t is easy to read short sentences. Like this one! So write notes in short sentences. Use long sentences only when absolutely essential. Information in long sentences is difficult to understand. Long sentences also slow down reading speed.
8. **Once you finish writing in detail, do a short summary at the end.**	**S**ounds like a lot of work, right? But believe it or not, this will make you jump with joy during exams. When you are rushed, summaries ensure *quick revision*. To apply the suggestions in this chapter, prepare notes in three parts: 1. **Outline** 2. **Body** 3. **Summary**

The outline helps you to know *at a glance* what information the notes contain and which questions you can answer. It also guides you to prepare the 'body' of the notes efficiently. The body gives you *full details* of each topic. The summary helps you make *quick* revisions of the topic.

While recalling information on a topic, just recall the outline or summary and you will be able to easily recall the entire information in the body!

9. Prepare a list of key points, formulas, and other important words.

This list is a lifesaver during exams. To prepare this easily look for all the important words, points, formulas, laws or definitions in the entire lesson. Then write them down one by one, preferably in short sentences.

If you make this list after preparing detailed notes, you will do this easily.

This list is different from the outline or summary; it contains *only* important points covering the *entire* lesson.

When you prepare notes using methods explained in this chapter, you get a POWERFUL benefit:

You will learn your topic thoroughly!

By the time you finish writing the outline, body and summary of your lesson, plus a list of all the important points, you will understand everything so thoroughly that you will never forget it!

If you don't have time to prepare detailed notes, at least prepare a list of important points and words. It will help you during revision and the exams.

10. Create your own questions. Write down all questions that can be asked on the topic.

After writing notes, put down all the questions that can be asked on the topic. These questions help in learning and stimulate your brain to think about the right answers. Also, exam papers are always full of questions! So writing questions that can be asked on the topic will give you an idea of what you can expect in the exams.

You can get many questions from these sources:

- ✦ Questions given at the end of the chapter in your textbook or other books
- ✦ Question papers of previous tests and exams
- ✦ Questions asked by teachers in class

Besides these, prepare more questions on your own. It will certainly help during the exams.

11. Use your favourite colour to highlight key points, headlines, and sub-headlines.

There is a big advantage of using colours in preparing notes. Colours help in better *registration* or recording of information in your brain—so you remember more easily. This is because colours involve more areas of your brain in recording that information, especially the right hemisphere.

Research on the brain shows that when information is recorded on a large area, it is remembered *more easily and for a longer time*!

So put this trick into practise. Write key words, headlines or sub-headlines in your favourite colour. Also, don't forget to highlight topics declared important by your teacher.

Now your notes will look attractive and complete. You will feel the desire to read it again and again!

12. Always leave blank space at the end of each topic in your notes.

Despite writing detailed notes, leave some blank space at the end of each lesson in your notes.

You can use this blank space for:

- **New ideas**—when you revise your notes next time, you might get new ideas that you can write in the blank space.
- **More information**—you might later get some new information or examples from your teacher, friends or other books.
- **Cross-references**—you can use this blank space to write about cross-references, other notes or textbooks that give additional information on this topic.
- **Corrections**—while reading your notes next time, if you find any mistake, you can write the correct answer in the blank space.

13. Keep notes in a safe place. You will need it for exams and job interviews, *if you are completing college.*

This is important. If you lose notes, you will be in deep trouble. Most students spend much time in searching for papers and books they have misplaced. But you can avoid this frustrating habit by learning to be more organised.

Keep all notes in a fixed place at home: on your study table, bookshelf or inside table drawers. Or even inside a box! And whenever you take the notes for reading, keep it back in the same place.

∞

CHAPTER 14

6 Secrets to Maintain Good Relations with Classmates

1. Smile and say *"hi"* to everyone you come across.

Your classmates are an important part of your study success and student life. They can help you:

- Solve study problems.
- Get the information you missed in class or practicals.
- When you fall ill or face any problem at school or college.
- Enjoy your student life more. After all, you spend many hours each day with classmates!

So it is a smart idea to maintain good relations with *all classmates. You never know whom you might need and when.*

The best way to do this is to smile cheerfully and say "hi" to everyone you come across. Make this a habit and you will enjoy good relations not only with classmates, but also other people *throughout life.*

2. Be friendly with all but be a close friend to few.

It is not possible to have a great friendship with everyone. Each person is different and you may not feel comfortable with everyone.

So choose a few classmates who are *good students* and maintain close friendship with them.

However, be nice to *everyone* in class. Never antagonize anyone. Each of us is unique. Learn to tolerate differences. This is a skill you will need most in life, whether you opt for a job or business in future.

So use classmates to master the *skill of maintaining good relations with everyone* and lay a solid foundation for BIG SUCCESS in life.

3. **Be there when they need you.** *Then they'll be with you when you need them...*

Especially when you need notes! Life need not be difficult if we learn to help each other. Help your classmates whenever they need you. Try your best to solve their problems, as much as you can. Then they will be more than ready to help when you need them.

4. **Listen when they speak. Share their happiness and sorrow.**

We all love people who listen when we speak, who are ready to laugh with us. We want to meet such people again and again. That's why you can make classmates happy and maintain good relations by listening when they speak. Be quiet and pay attention when they narrate their experiences. Share their happiness and sorrow.

Listening well while others speak is a very important skill that will help you achieve more success and popularity in career, business and life in general.

So use opportunities of conversations with friends to cultivate this great habit of *listening attentively.*

5. **Don't gossip, quarrel or argue.**

This leads to tension and problems! So avoid such troublesome activities. Also stay away from friends who gossip.

If you cannot avoid such friends, draw their attention to something else when they gossip. Ask questions on studies that are mutually helpful or enjoyable. This is the best way to divert attention.

6. **Find out if your friends have problems with studies, then help them to solve those problems.**

How many students are there who do not have some problems with studies? Almost none! Most students have some weakness in one subject or the other.

So ask your friends if they have any study problems or find any topic difficult to understand. Then help your friends with those topics. Helping classmates to solve their problems is the quickest way to make them appreciate you. Use every opportunity to teach others. *Teaching others is the best way to master your studies!*

We regularly use this method in schools or training sessions to turn low performers into high achievers.

How does it work? When you teach others, you become more interested in learning that topic better. *You start thinking like a teacher*—you wonder how you can explain the topic better so that classmates will understand it easily. When you think in this manner, you not only teach your friends better, but also understand the topic better.

You too can discuss *your* study problems with friends. And make learning a really enjoyable activity—by using the *"Teach Each Other"* method.

∞

CHAPTER 15

6 Secrets to Choose a Good Tutor

1. **Check his or her background and performance.**

   If you wish to attend tuition or private coaching classes or want to hire a home tutor, you need to check their background. After all, you will be investing money and time on your tutor. So ensure you get proper value for your investment.

   The magnitude of your academic success also depends on the quality of the tutor you engage. So check out the tutor's experience, qualification, and quality of teaching before committing to the service.

2. **If possible, meet your tutor's previous students.**

   The best way to find a good tutor is via satisfied students. Try to meet previous students of the tutor you want to hire.

   Take help from senior students, classmates or other friends in this task. They might know someone who may have studied under this tutor.

   While hiring a home tutor, ask for references or experience. Remember, you are paying for the tutor's service. So choose a good one.

3. **Your tutor's fees should be affordable.**

   Don't burn a hole in your or your parents' pocket, unless you have no other option. Usually, you will find some good tutors who charge reasonable rates as tuition fees. Search for such tutors! Talk with friends, classmates, or relatives, and ask if they know any such tutors or coaching classes.

   Some teachers in your school or college may be taking private tuitions at their home. Find out about such teachers; they usually charge lower fees than coaching classes.

   Also, do not be afraid to accept the services of new tutors whose academic qualification are good and fees lower. Make extensive enquiries before going to a high-charging tutor or coaching class.

4. **Ensure your tutor takes regular tests and gives you feedback on your performance.**

   Just understanding a topic is not enough. Practise expressing what you learn in writing and orally. Such practice comes with giving tests and model exams.

   So before hiring a tutor or joining a coaching class, check whether they conduct regular tests. These tests help you to get feedback on your learning and ability to deal with exams.

5. **Your tutor should know the art of explaining well. And you should be able to understand what s/he is teaching.**

   It's no use joining a tuition class or hiring a home tutor if you can't understand what they are teaching.

   A good tutor knows how to explain well so that students understand easily. Ensure you get such tutor. The only way to do this is to meet the previous students of that tutor. Or ask friends if they know any such good tutor.

   Besides, some tuition or coaching centres allow you to attend classes for few days without fees or after paying a nominal advance. Attending such classes gives you an idea of how they teach and helps you take a final decision.

6. **Your tutor must complete your course and not vanish midway.**

   We know this sounds shocking. But such things do happen. You can avoid this by checking facts. Since how many years is the tutor teaching? Does s/he take classes regularly and till the term ends? Answers to these questions will help you take the right decision.

   Unfortunately, if your tutor stops taking classes midway, don't get upset. Find out if your tutor has any problems, like health or family problems. If possible, wait till your tutor overcomes these problems, then restart classes.

   Meanwhile, take help from friends, teachers or parents to master your studies. And keep your head cool. Or find another tutor!

   ∞

CHAPTER 16

7 Secrets to Make Your Study Place Perfect

1. Choose a proper study place.

To a large extent, your study place determines your study success! So choose your study place carefully. For better results, your study place should be:

- Comfortable
- Free of distraction

In other words, your study place should *invite* you to study.

A separate chair and table is the best place for studying. But don't study in bed. You may fall asleep. Also, don't study at the kitchen table. Your stomach might start rumbling!

If possible, it is best to use a separate room for studying. If you can't get a separate room, create an enclosed space by using curtains.

TV, a music system, comics, novels, noise, etc. are enemies of studies and easily distract you. Show them the door.

2. Sit comfortably. Good posture allows the brain better blood circulation and ensures better learning.

You can study for longer periods easily, without strain, only if you sit comfortably. Many students suffer backaches, shoulder or neck pain because they do not sit properly. So ensure you are comfortable and the posture is correct.

To ensure better posture, select a chair that supports the lower back. Also, your feet should easily touch the floor when you sit on the chair.

All this ensures three main benefits:

- Better blood circulation for body and brain
- Better oxygen supply too
- Less strain or tension on your body

Better blood circulation and oxygen supply makes the brain work at its *optimum level*. You can learn better and master study material faster.

3. Keep your study place properly ventilated.

Open the windows. Let fresh air enter. Fresh air keeps the mind alert and kicking—so necessary to help you concentrate better on studies.

There is another advantage of proper ventilation—you get air with *more oxygen*. When you breathe such air, your brain gets its pet food—oxygen. With enough oxygen supply your brain will work at top speed and help you learn better.

A key point: if you have the habit of frequently looking out of the open window, put a curtain on the lower half of the window. Keep the upper half open. Now you'll have fresh air and no distraction.

4. Keep the study room temperature cool. It will keep you comfortable and awake!

Even the room temperature of your study place is important. It influences mood and concentration. A cool room is better; a warm one can make you feel sleepy.

Also, extreme cold or hot temperature isn't good either. They steal your efficiency. But this doesn't mean you should check the temperature every time you study!

The important thing is: just *be comfortable*. If it's too cold, wear warm clothes. If it's too hot, turn on the fan or the cooler.

5. Proper lighting is important.

The source of light should be above eye level, behind or to your left and of proper intensity.

How do you check the intensity of light? It is right if you can COMFORTABLY read the smallest textbook print. Yet, see to it that the intensity of light is on the *brighter side*.

Proper lighting is important as the eyes get strained easily if you study in dim light. Constant eyestrain may affect eyesight. Also, you cannot concentrate properly with poor lighting.

So take preventive steps and arrange better lighting in your study place.

6. Display goal cards, timetable, important dates, and positive messages around your study place.

This is the best secret to make your study place motivating, inspiring and inviting! Displaying these things near your study place is an *effective way* to programme your brain to help you achieve "great success in studies" on a TOP priority basis.

So paste positive messages, goal cards, important dates, etc. on the wall near your study table. Once displayed, look at them with love and expectation—especially before starting each session and during breaks.

Expect to succeed with ease. The brain makes your expectations come true.

7. Keep everything ready and available to avoid irritation and prevent loss of focus.

How do you feel when you don't find a thing you need? Irritated and frustrated, isn't it? In addition, you lose concentration and search for that missing thing. Then you lose time, energy and focus.

Avoid this by: keeping sharpened pencils, erasers, pens, highlighters, rulers, compass box, paper, notes, textbook, dictionary, and atlas in your study room—*near your study table*.

Now you won't have to pull your hair in frustration when you need things! *So be organized*.

∞

CHAPTER 17

6 Secrets to Read Faster and Understand Better

1. First find your present reading speed. It will help you know how much your speed has increased when you use a fast-reading aid.

You can increase, even double, reading speed. Imagine the advantages! If you need an hour to learn a topic at present, you could then learn it in half an hour!

Before learning to increase your reading speed, first check out your present speed. Then you will know the exact improvement made.

Here's a simple way to check reading speed: Read text in one minute at your *normal* speed. Then count the *number of words* you read. That's your reading speed in 'words per minute'.

2. Use this simple reading aid to increase speed.

There are three main reasons for slow reading:
- Stopping your eyes at every word while reading.
- Reading word by word.
- Moving your eyes back to read the previous words again and again.

Such actions consume much time. The only way to correct them—*move your eyes smoothly and at a faster pace over the lines in your book*. Then your reading speed will increase tremendously.

How do you move your eyes smoothly? By using a 'fast-reading aid'—a pen, pencil, or even your finger! Next, choose any text and read by moving your 'fast-reading aid' (pen, pencil or finger) below the lines you are reading, for a minute. Then count the number of words you have read.

You will find an improvement *because your eyes do not get a chance to stop at every word and shift backwards*. Some students have achieved 50 to 100 per cent improvement in reading speed with this simple method. After some practise you can read faster even without using any 'fast-reading aid'.

The next fast-reading trick will help you further increase reading speed and the ability to understand.

3. **Read words in groups, not word by word.**

    Learn to read words in groups by training your eyes to see more than one word at a glance. For example, read the group of words marked below in a single glance. Stop your eyes on the underlined letter in each group, which is approximately the centre of the group of words.

    (You know) (how to) (read faster).

    In this way, practise reading two or more words at a glance. Do such practise for only 2-3 minutes daily. You will soon learn the technique.

    You can use newspaper columns for this. As such columns are of 4 to 6 words only, try to read each line in one glance. That is, move your eyes from top to bottom along the column and not horizontally. If your eyes are strained with this method, don't use it.

4. **Have a strong desire to read faster. Visualize yourself reading faster.**

    Reading is mostly mental work. Therefore, you can use visualization to read faster. *Here's how*: close your eyes, and imagine yourself reading faster. Picture yourself reading a book and moving your head from left to right, smoothly and quickly—to indicate you are reading faster.

    Do this visualization for 2-3 minutes, whenever you have time. Especially before practising the actual methods recommended in this chapter.

5. **Increase word power to increase reading speed and grasping power too.**

    Word power plays a powerful role in increasing reading speed.

    Learn the meaning and pronunciation of words that are **frequently** used in your study course. Bingo! Your reading speed will accelerate! Not only this, you will also understand your subjects easily!

    Even mastering thousand *basic words* makes reading and understanding easier. Basic words are ones used frequently in textbooks, magazines and newspapers.

    You can also do this thing: while reading any book or newspaper, mark the word you don't understand or can't pronounce properly. Then look it up in the dictionary.

    Also make a list of such words and check them frequently, recall their meaning, and try to use those words while speaking and writing.

    Make this a habit to increase your word power; this will automatically increase your reading speed! Also, your grasping power and ability to concentrate will get a big boost because reading at higher speed prevents stray thoughts.

6. Practise, practise, practise...

Faster reading comes with practise. So read, read, read... with fast-reading aids. Measure your reading speed at monthly intervals.

Measuring reading speed at regular interval shows whether you are improving or not. If you are not, start all over again.

Aim for a speed of 150 to 250 words per minute. More the merrier!

∞

CHAPTER 18

13 Secrets to Study Better and Smarter

1. Find your ALERT TIME ZONE. This is the time when the brain is fresh, alert and eager to work.

In this time zone, you will learn more in less time. And remember more. Your 'alert time' zone can be early morning, if you are an early bird. Or it could be late night, if you are a night owl! Find your best time and use it more.

However, there are three big advantages if you study in the early morning:

- You have more energy to study.
- As your body and mind have been rested during sleep, you will remember better.
- No TV, no phone, no talking. You will face fewer disturbances at this time, as others will be still sleeping.

So use early morning hours to study difficult or important subjects.

2. Open your book with interest. Ask questions to 'switch on' your brain.

As you open a book, tell yourself, *"I love to learn as better learning leads to better living."*

Ask yourself: Where have I heard this topic before? What benefits will I get from studying it? Asking such questions acts as a warm-up exercise for your brain and creates a *desire* to learn. Usually, you learn something from every topic. That's why it is included in your syllabus.

Remember, your brain works **efficiently** when you have the interest and desire to learn better. And you can increase your interest in studies by keeping this slogan in mind...

Better Learning→Rich Living

Yes, better learning leads to rich living. It can open the way to a high-paying career, a rich lifestyle and happy living for me. So I give TOP priority to learning. I feel strong desire to study.

Copy this slogan on a stiff card or on the back of a visiting card and paste it on the wall near your study place where you can see it.

3. Before you begin reading, glance through the study material.

This is one of the smart secrets to study better. Don't jump into the topic the moment you open a book. First glance through the entire topic for few seconds. Read headlines, sub-headlines, lists, tables, and check sketches or pictures, if any.

There are three main benefits:
- A rough outline of the lesson is created in your brain.
- When you read the lesson in detail, it is recorded in your brain alongwith the outline formed at the start. This helps in better organization of information in your brain—which aids stronger memorisation.
- You will know what to *expect* when you read the lesson. So you will understand and learn the lesson easily.

This method is very important for better learning and strong memory. So use it regularly until it becomes a habit.

4. If there are questions at the end of lessons, read them first.

The brain becomes restless when questions enter it; then it automatically tries to find answers! With questions whirling inside it, the brain recognizes answers easily when you read a lesson in detail.

This is an **effective study method** as it helps to:
- Stimulate your brain to learn more
- Saves much time and effort
- Helps you understand better
- Helps you remember easily

So before reading a lesson, *read the questions first.*

5. Study properly. Understand thoroughly.

When you read study material, pay full attention and understand things properly. Keep a pencil handy to underline important words and sentences.

Also, mark difficult or doubtful words or sentences. Then use a dictionary or reference book or ask your teacher to explain this. Do not accumulate doubts. *Clear them on the same day.*

This habit itself will make you a brilliant student. So always practise it to stay ahead of others!

6. Recite, revise, summarise!

A single reading won't help you learn better. Also, mere recitation like a parrot is not good either.

The best way to study is:

- First read a few paragraphs of the lesson and understand them.
- Then recite, revise or read those paragraphs again—once or twice, as required. In this way, read the entire lesson.
- Finally, write a quick summary of the lesson in your own words.

The above style of studying help you remember lessons for a much longer time. This is because you do many things together: reading, understanding, reciting, and writing!

7. Test yourself. Close the book and answer questions after you have read the chapter.

Very few students do this. It is very important because testing yourself while studying helps in three ways:

- You make an instant revision.
- You know how much you have understood.
- You have quick practice for a test or exam.

You can do this testing after reading a lesson, reciting it, or after writing a summary.

To test yourself, use questions at the end of the textbook. If there are no questions, make up your own ones related to the topic and answer them. For example, quickly create your questions with these standard ones: Where is it found? Why or how is it used? What is its importance? What is its function? What are the advantages? Etc.

Also answer questions asked by teachers in class. And if you can get question papers of previous tests or exams, answer them too.

8. Give yourself a five-minute break after every 30 minutes' study.

Many students have the habit of studying for a long time without a break. This is a bad habit because:

- It decreases focus or concentration over time.
- Slows down learning speed and efficiency.
- Strains and tenses your body.

Therefore, take a break for five minutes after every half an hour. This gives your body *and brain* rest. Your brain works best when you give it frequent rest as it uses this to complete the learning process by forming new neuronal networks.

During the five-minute break, don't read anything else. Just stretch, take a few deep breaths, close your eyes, and relax. This recharges your brain and body with fresh energy, so you learn more without strain.

9. Identify key points and remember them.

We have frequently referred to 'key points'. What does this mean? A key point is the base, the *main idea*, on which a paragraph is built. Every well-written paragraph contains only one or two main ideas.

Words or sentences that answer questions like 'what' or 'why' usually form the main idea in a paragraph. Identify them and you have the key points.

Underline such key points. **Learn and remember** them well, because key points help you write good answers. They are also useful for quick revisions. You will learn how to revise in the next chapter.

10. To understand better, use examples. If possible, create your own examples.

It is easy to understand any topic if an example is given. That's why most books contain examples to explain the topic. So while learning lessons ensure you refer to examples. You will understand quickly.

Sometimes, teachers also give good examples while teaching. Write them down in your notebook and use them while studying. If possible, create your own examples by looking at the practical use of that topic in day-to-day life.

11. When studying physics, understand the laws and theories properly. Memorize formulas, symbols, and units.

Every subject is unique so you have to use different study techniques for each. Physics is almost like mathematics. It mainly consists of laws, theories and problems.

To master physics properly, study it in this way:

- Carefully read and understand the laws, formulas and theories till they are crystal clear.
- Memorize symbols, units, and formulas used in physics problems.
- Practise all types of problems, until you can solve them easily.

However, if you feel physics is difficult, there may be a big reason behind this: *lack of understanding of the* <u>*basics*</u>.

Understand the basics and it will be easier to learn. This is the best secret for any difficult subject: **master the basics.**

How do you master the basics? By revising your old books or notes. For example, if you are in the 10th standard, revise physics books of the 8th and 9th standard.

Do such revisions during holidays or vacations. Especially revise previous lessons *related* to lessons of this year.

Mastering the basics ensures two big benefits: you score better in the exams and lay a solid foundation for excellent performance in the next year.

12. **While studying chemical reactions, do not just memorize them. Understand why the reaction is taking place and why a particular product is formed.**

Chemistry is easy. And if you follow the above secret it will be easier. To understand and remember difficult chemical reactions or formulas, use this trick: write them down in a chart and check them frequently. You can also hang that chart on the wall near your study table.

Once you learn the reactions/formulas thoroughly, make another chart with new chemical reactions and hang this in place of the previous chart.

Try to recognise chemistry being applied in daily life and in things around you—in the bathroom, kitchen, and almost everywhere! This creates more interest in chemistry and helps you learn better.

For example, chemistry plays a role in daily use items—soap, detergents, perfumes, acids, and preservatives. When you see a practical application of things you are studying, you will learn and remember more.

13. **While studying biology, keep looking at related diagrams. You will learn text and diagrams at the same time.**

This is a smart trick to learn biology quickly. By looking at diagrams, you can understand text easily.

Also, diagrams and pictures, especially coloured ones, help to remember information more strongly. This is because pictures involve the brain's right hemisphere in learning, which results in recording of the lesson on a *larger area* of the brain. When data is recorded on larger area, you remember it more strongly.

Also, during exams if you just recall the diagram, you can easily remember the related description.

However, if there is no diagram, based on the description in your lesson, create your own rough diagram. This helps you understand better and remember more.

This is how you make big success easy to achieve.

Do what ordinary students don't do!

∞

CHAPTER 19

2 Secrets to Revise Effectively

1. Use a smart revision schedule and cut down the time and effort required to master studies.

Experiments have shown that most students forget about 80 per cent of what they learn within 24 hours. Sounds like a horror story? To avoid being a victim, use this smart revision schedule:

- **1st revision:** When you finish learning a new lesson, revise it immediately, within ten minutes of the first learning it.
- **2nd revision:** Revise again before going to bed on the same day or next morning.

The two revisions are essential to remember better. After this, you can revise once a week, then once a month, or as frequently as you need, till the exams. Revise difficult lessons more frequently.

All this sounds like too much revision. But since the time gap between each revision is less, you can do it quickly, learn better, and score higher! So start using it NOW.

2. Use correct revision techniques to save time and effort.

You don't have to read your entire lesson word for word every time you revise, *if you have understood it clearly.*

Just glance through each page and quickly read important points, sentences or key words.

You can do this quick revision, if you have prepared good notes or a list of keywords or 'mind map notes' (you will learn this in the chapter '11 Secrets to Multiply Memory Power'.)

Also, look at the sketch, table or graph, if given during revision. You can also practise the diagram by drawing it quickly. Similarly, you can solve some maths or physics problems as practise.

But remember, you can do fast revision of important points or other information only when you follow this revision schedule. If you learn a new lesson today and revise it after a few weeks or months, you will not remember it as much. And you will have to study the entire lesson again, which requires more time and effort!

So follow the smart revision schedule and save time and energy.

∞

CHAPTER 20

5 Secrets to Solve Maths Problems

1. Before starting a new type of problem, revise the basics, if any.

Yes, solving new maths problem try to understand the basics involved. Then you can solve these easily.

Most students fail in maths due to one reason: *not mastering the basics*. As said earlier, you can solve problems by revising the previous years' syllabus. It sounds like much work. But remember, all you have to do is just read old lessons *related* to the new maths problem. It only takes a few minutes or hours.

By avoiding this simple action, students accumulate doubts and the subject grows tougher each day.

You need not suffer this problem. Be wise, get your doubts cleared by referring to old lessons or ask friends or teachers to help you. If your basic knowledge of maths is strong, you can deal with any problem. So don't live with weaknesses.

2. Never memorize problems. Understand the concept. Only memorize formulas and units.

The big advantage of maths is you don't have to memorize anything, except for formulas and units. But to become an expert, there is only one way: *lots of practise.*

The more you practise solving a particular type of problem, the more *proficient* you become in solving those problems.

When you practise:

- Your brain automatically records how to solve a problem and the steps used.
- Your speed increases and you can solve problems more quickly.
- Your confidence increases, helping you solve problems in exams more calmly and efficiently.

So practise well. The best way to do this is to solve all problems in your textbooks. Also solve problems given by your teacher. Once you do these, find question papers of previous years' exams to solve.

3. **When your teacher solves a problem in class, write it in your notebook exactly as your teacher has done.**

In solving maths problems, the steps are as important as arriving at the correct solution.

So when your teacher explains how to solve problems, pay attention and copy all the steps in your notebook—in exactly the same order your teacher is doing.

Otherwise, you might later forget some steps. This may cause confusion. Then you might lose marks in the exams for not following all the steps.

4. **Do your maths homework as soon as possible, while the instructions are still fresh in the brain.**

As explained earlier, doing homework on the same day is very helpful because the lessons are *still fresh* in the mind. So you can easily remember all instructions, information and steps you have learnt. You can then do homework easily, in lesser time.

Although this advice applies to all subjects, it is more important for maths. If you postpone maths homework, you might forget various steps used to solve problems. Especially if you find maths difficult.

So following this simple secret of *doing your maths homework promptly* will make maths easier for you, even if you now find it tough.

To make maths easier, do more than asked! That is, solve more problems than the teacher asks. This additional work helps fix the formulas, steps and principles involved *more firmly* in your brain. If you keep doing this, day by day maths will get easier!

5. **If confused, have your doubts cleared IMMEDIATELY or on the same day!**

Unlike languages, mathematics is a subject in which you can score even 100 per cent!

So study it properly. Don't accumulate confusions and doubts. Take help from teachers, friends, or tutors and understand the concept properly.

And *practise a lot*; then you will enjoy mathematics and also score higher.

∞

CHAPTER 21

11 Secrets to Multiply Memory Power

1. **Believe 100 per cent in your memory power.**

   Your brain records all thoughts, feelings, actions, and reactions. If you repeatedly think you can't remember better or learn quickly, your brain records these thoughts also. Then it takes steps to make this real. In other words, you don't remember well. You don't learn quickly.

   So start thinking **you can** remember everything you learn. Think this repeatedly. **Expect** to remember. Think such positive thoughts repeatedly using the affirmation method, and instruct your brain to improve your memory power.

   Here are two affirmations to use daily to instruct the brain to make your memory stronger. Repeat the affirmations given below several times daily.

   + *Day by day my memory is getting better and better.*
   + *My brain is perfect. I remember everything I learn.*

2. **Remember the three stages to better memory: *Registration, Retention,* and *Recall*.**

   REGISTRATION is *recording* information you want to remember in your brain. Better concentration, more oxygenated blood, a balanced diet, deep interest in studies, etc. all help the brain in strong registration.

   RETENTION is storing information in your brain. It is stored in the form of a neuronal network (a network of brain cells called neurons). Concentration, **revision**, rest or sleep help in better storage.

   RECALL is recollecting information in your brain for use. This becomes easy when new information is stored by **linking** it to old information. This is called **association**. When you recall old information, new things you have learnt keep coming out.

   For example, when you learn about a new species of plant and think, 'Hey, this looks similar to a plant in my garden,' then you are associating a new plant (new information) to the one in your garden (old information). So when you remember the plant in your garden, you will easily remember information about the new plant too.

For better registration, retention and recall, use the proper study methods and revision schedules.

3. To remember better, start study sessions in a relaxed state.

This is the most simple secret to improve memory. If you start studies in a relaxed state of mind and body, you will be able to *easily* pay attention to studies. And you will remember more. In a relaxed state, there is less work for your brain and it can spare more energy to record what you study!

From today onwards, spare a few minutes to relax before studies. Use this simple technique to relax:

- Sit comfortably in your chair.
- Take a few slow, deep breaths.
- As you breathe out slowly, feel as if your body has become light and relaxed.
- Repeat the above slow, deep breathing three or four times.

Now begin studying. You can repeat this relaxation process at the beginning of *each* study session and during short study breaks.

4. Emotionalise your study topic.

Emotions **increase** activity of the brain cells. They help create a strong impression on the brain—which leads to better memory. So to improve memory and remember more, feel emotional about your subject.

How do you become emotional? Use affirmations. We have given an affirmation to help you pour emotion into your topic! Say this affirmation *with intense feeling* before studying maths:

> "I *love* maths. It is *so* interesting.
> It is very useful in day-to-day life
> and also in building my career."

Ridiculous? Believe it or not, this works. Because it helps you *feel good* about maths. It helps to create interest and positive feelings in your mind. All these positive emotions stimulate the brain to record better and remember more. Repeat this affirmation regularly. Use it for other subjects also.

While studying other subjects, simply replace the word 'maths' with the subject you are studying. *And remember*: feel *strong love* for that subject when you say the affirmation. Even acting "as if you love it" works! Besides, when you can't avoid the subjects, why not love them?!

5. **To remember important or difficult topics, LINK your topic with something funny or weird. Exaggerate the things you need to remember.**

    Suppose you are studying a chemical reaction where two chemicals are mixed to create a new product. Imagine pouring those two chemicals into a big red cauldron that produces spluttering noises and ejects the new product onto the ground.

    Weird, isn't it? But this will help you remember the chemical reaction easily. Absurd or silly things make a strong impression on your brain. When you link not-so-interesting things with funny ones, all you need do is just remember the funny thing, and you will also remember the not-so-interesting thing!

    So put this secret into practise. You will need it very much because most of what you study is not so interesting—*but compulsory!* So to remember difficult topics use all these tricks: Link your study topics with...

    + Funny things or outrageous incidents
    + Weird, strange things or incidents
    + Interesting stories or jokes

6. **To avoid memory problems get good sleep. Sleep for 8 hours.**

    Believe it or not, good sleep improves memory! Research on the brain shows that when we are asleep, our brain processes new information we have learnt and stores them in long-term memory. Information stored in long-term memory is remembered better.

    Research also shows that our brain needs 8 hours of sleep to work properly, and to stay fit and efficient. So sleep 8 hours and boost your memory power effortlessly!

    In fact, use this trick for more advantage: read new lessons or difficult topics before sleeping. Then revise it again next morning when you wake up. You will understand and remember it more easily.

    You can use this trick during daytime too. After studying for some time, rest or sleep for a short period. This will help you remember better.

Make sure you study regularly and finish most of your studies much before the exam begins, so that you can sleep for 8 hours even during exams.

7. Use cards, charts and posters to make strong and better registrations in the brain.

It is easy to remember cards, charts and posters prepared in *attractive colours* because they register strongly in the brain.

So use colourful cards, charts or posters of:

- Important formulas
- Crucial dates
- Grammar rules
- Key points of important topics, etc.

Use colour sketch pens and good quality paper or sheets to prepare cards, charts or poster. This is important.

However, you can prepare them in any size. You can make them smaller and keep them on your study table so that you can look at them frequently.

Or you can prepare them in a larger size, write all important information in attractive colours and hang them on the wall near your study table. Look at it *frequently*. Then the information in the poster will be firmly embedded in your brain.

All these smart actions help you remember more.

8. Learn to prepare and use 'Mind-map Notes'.

Making mind-map notes involves the brain 100% and helps you remember information easily. They look funny but are easy to prepare. See a simple example below.

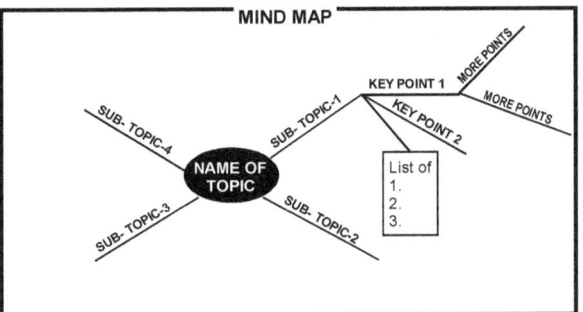

Start by writing the name of the subject in the centre of the page. Then write the main sub-topics around it. Then branch out key points from each sub-topic. The lines drawn need not be straight lines. Draw them in free hand in any shape or in any direction!

Add related points or minor points under the main points. You can add formulae, examples, pictures and symbols in boxes under sub-topics.

There are no rigid rules in preparing mind-maps. **Just be creative** and prepare it any way you like. Use colours to make it attractive and unique.

In the end, the mind-map will show all important KEY POINTS on *one page*. At a single glance, you can see all the important points of your lesson. This helps you remember easily and revise quickly! So start preparing and using mind-map notes.

9. **If you have a problem remembering important dates or names use this simple trick: create *funny sentences* using names or dates you want to remember.**

This is a time-tested secret to better recall. Remembering funny sentences is easy because we all love funny things. When you recall that funny sentence you created, you automatically remember information *linked to it*.

Also, when you link information with funny a sentence, it is recorded on a large area of the brain. So you remember it more strongly.

For example, to remember planets in our solar system—Mercury, Venus, Earth, Mars, Jupiter, Saturn, Uranus, Neptune, Pluto—*in that order* you can use this funny sentence:

Miss **V**enus **E**arned **M**ore by **J**ust **S**elling **a U**sed **N**ecklace to **P**riya.

Based on this example, you can create your own sentences that are funny and easy to remember. Similar sentences can be created and used to remember difficult things or topics.

10. **Use memory aids like mnemonics to remember important words, lists, or other information.**

The funny sentence you just read to remember planets in our solar system is actually based on a mnemonics principle.

Mnemonics are useful memory aids. There are many types of mnemonics. *Acronym* is one such kind of mnemonic that is very popular. Acronyms are words formed by using the *first letter* of words you want to remember.

A simple example of an Acronym is VIBGYOR—to indicate seven colours in the spectrum—**V**iolet, **I**ndigo, **B**lue, **G**reen, **Y**ellow, **O**range, and **R**ed.

Similarly, you can use acronyms to remember tough study material easily. Just take the first letter of the words or data you want to remember and create a word or words using those letters. You can use this trick to remember list of names or keywords, etc.

11. Use the Link System to remember a long list of things in a specific order.

The Link System is another popular mnemonic method to help you remember things or events in a specific order.

In the Link System, use your imagination and make a mental picture using all the things you have to remember. Link those with **funny, huge, colourful, absurd** and **unusual** pictures to recall better.

For example, let's see how to use the Link System to remember ten things in the given order:

1. Car
2. Teacher
3. Pen
4. Book
5. Shirt
6. Umbrella
7. Camera
8. Wheelchair
9. Torch
10. Hat

Now apply the Link System in the following way:

- You are going to college driving your big **car**.
- On the way you visit your **teacher**'s house, ask him to sit on the top of your car along with his blackboard. Then you begin driving.
- On the way the teacher begins writing on the blackboard with a big white **pen**.
- He opens a big unusual **book** for reference and again begins to write.
- As the blackboard is full, he removes his **shirt** and uses it as a duster and cleanes the board.
- It starts to rain, so the teacher opens his colourful big **umbrella**, ties it to his head and again begins writing furiously, as you drive towards college.
- Sensing this as a rare photographic opportunity, a photographer quickly pulls out his **camera.**
- He grabs a **wheelchair**, hooks it to the car, gets on the chair, and begins taking pictures.
- As the light becomes dull due to cloudy skies, the photographer takes out a huge **torch**, switches it on and focuses it on the teacher.
- The sudden bright light shockes the teacher; he quickly coveres his face with his **hat**!

Crazy, isn't it? That's exactly why you will remember information easily when you link them together by using **funny** things or situations.

Also imagine those things in brilliant colours, unusual shapes or sizes. You will never forget it.

∞

CHAPTER 22

8 Secrets to Make Difficult Subjects Easy

1. **Stop putting up with difficult subjects. Identify them and take action to make them easy.**

   There is no such thing as a difficult subject. It is all YOUR creation! You make subjects difficult by:
   + Paying little attention to them
   + Giving them less time
   + Ignoring the basics for years
   + Calling them boring, dull, useless!

   Now is the time to transform them from difficult to easy. How? First identify the difficult subjects. This is simple—the subjects in which you *consistently* score less are your tough subjects.

2. **Spend less time on TV and other unimportant activities and use this time to make tough subjects easy.**

   Don't groan! This is temporary. Reduce the time you spend on TV or other less important activities and **use the time you save for studies and paying more attention to difficult subjects.**

   For example, if you spend 2 hours watching TV each day, reduce it to an hour.

   If you spend 7 hours each week going out with friends, cut it down to 2 or 3 hours.

   Similarly, if there are household chores you do, finish them off quickly or ask someone else in your home to do them and save your time.

3. **Master the basics of tough subjects AS FAST AS YOU CAN.**

   This is one of the best secrets to make difficult subjects easy. When students do not understand the basics or previous lessons of a particular subject, that subject *continues* to grow tougher each day! Stop this within a few days with two tricks:
   + Spend a few minutes to identify tough areas or topics of your difficult subjects and clear those areas with the help of friends, teachers, tutors or parents.

For example, let us assume that Maths is your difficult subject. Now if you check your maths textbook carefully, you will realize that *all* the maths lessons are not difficult. You will find some lessons are easier, while others are difficult. Mark the difficult lessons. And take the help of others to *understand* and practise them. Soon these lessons will also become easy. That is, the *entire maths* subject will become easy!

Similarly, if you find English grammar difficult, find out and mark exactly which lessons you find difficult. Then take the help of others to understand and learn it properly.

- Go through textbooks of previous classes. Revise definitions, rules, and other information related to your tough subjects. Once basic concepts are cleared, you can easily understand the present lessons.

4. **Don't worry if you can't revise the previous syllabus in one go. Do it whenever you come across difficult topics.**

It is not necessary for you to revise the previous year's textbooks in one sitting. It may not even be possible. It is better to clear your doubts as and when you come across a difficult topic.

For example, if you have been taught a new chemistry lesson today in class, and you did not understand it properly, refer to a chemistry textbook or notes of the last year or semester. And search for topics *related* to today's lesson. Then read it and you may understand today's lesson better.

Also, ensure you use proper:

- Study methods
- Revision schedules
- Memory improvement secrets, given in the earlier chapters.

By using all the methods *together*, you can make difficult subjects easy without sweat and tears.

5. **Build your own student friendly reference library to retain mastery of subjects.**

Collect all information or books to help you master difficult subjects. Look for subject-specific books. For example: 'Science kit' 'How to Improve English' etc.

Check for such books in your school, college or public library. Or check bookstores or the Internet. Ask your teachers, parents and friends if they know about such books.

Nowadays many student-friendly reference systems are available. For example, 'Encyclopaedia for children', etc. If you can't procure such an encyclopaedia, don't worry. Build your own reference library at a fraction of the cost of an encyclopaedia, which will be more useful than any other reference system. How? Just collect textbooks of different subjects from standard 1 to 12!

If you don't need books on all subjects, collect *only* textbooks of subjects you find difficult. Now, whenever you don't understand a topic, simply open and read previous textbooks till things are clear. Such a collection can help you even if you are in college or appearing for competitive exams!

6. Seek help from brilliant friends and teachers, or engage special tutors. Grab hold of ANY weapon you can to conquer difficult subjects.

Please remember: if some subjects appear difficult, it is **not** because you are less intelligent than others. It is because you neglected them earlier.

*You can get rid of this weakness anytime **you** decide to do so.* Decide today.

Mark or list the things you don't understand. Then call your friends and ask them to explain those topics to you, whenever they are free. Or meet your teacher and discuss these topics. Take notes and revise till things become clear to you. Keep revising *till you master those difficult topics*.

You can also join coaching classes for subjects you find difficult—so that you can spend more time on them and learn better.

Alternatively, you can hire a home tutor, on an hourly basis, to either teach all the difficult subjects, or only teach lessons you find tough.

7. Audio record difficult topics and listen to recorded information after relaxing.

This is a 'modern' technique you can use to deal with difficult topics. Here's how:

✦ Put a blank cassette in the tape recorder and press the 'Record' button.

✦ Now record lessons of the difficult topic by *reading it slowly* in a normal voice. Hold the tape recorder close to the mouth to record your voice clearly. If you have an external mike, use it. Once you finish recording, keep the cassette in a safe place.

✦ Whenever you have time to study the difficult topic, do this: put the cassette in the recorder. Now sit comfortably near it. Close your eyes. Take 3-4 slow, deep breaths to relax. Then turn on the tape recorder and listen to the difficult topics. As you listen to your voice, keep your eyes closed.

As you are listening in a *relaxed* state of mind, you will learn difficult topics better. Hear the recording a few times till it becomes easy for you. Then try to remember key points and revise.

8. **To quickly make difficult subjects easy, teach it to others.**

This is the best trick. We all study properly when we have to teach others.

So get hold of a classmate who finds the same topic difficult and tell him, "Let us try to explain this topic to each other. Then we both will understand it better." Meet on a particular date and time.

Then teach that topic to your classmate. Also, ask your classmate to explain something that you do not understand about the topic.

Keep doing this; it really works. This is because we *think differently* when teaching others and understand points that initially appeared difficult.

If you can't find a classmate for this method, *there is an alternative*. First read the topic, then sit before a mirror, act as a teacher and explain the topic to yourself in the mirror! This method also works, provided you don't end up just staring at your face!

∞

CHAPTER 23

4 Secrets to Clear Backlog Quickly

1. The first step in solving any problem: identify it correctly.

Start by finding out *exactly* why you have not finished studies. Answer questions like:
- Is it because I did not start early?
- Is it because I find studying difficult or am less interested in studies?
- Is it since I waste time on unimportant things?
- Is there any other distracting factor?

So discover the *root cause* behind the backlog.

2. Now immediately start removing *that* root cause or causes.

Once you discover why you are lagging in studies, follow these simple steps:
- Note HOW you can remove the backlog. What actions can you take to complete studies?
- Write as many solutions you can think.
- Then choose the best solution.
- Write this solution on a card and keep it on your study table or paste it on the wall near your study table or bed.
- Keep acting on the best solution till that cause is removed and you finish doing all your study work.

These actions are simple yet practical and will help you clear your backlog. Besides, you can use the solutions in this and other chapters to make quick progress in studies.

Usually, the number one reason for lagging behind in studies is *lack of interest*. If this is true, use the earlier chapters on motivation and goal setting to develop more interest in studies.

3. **Allot a specific time to deal with backlog.**

   Aim to clear backlog as quickly as you can. This means "no-no" to TV, outings, phone calls, etc. until you are back in the race.

   So replace leisure activities in your timetable with activities to clear the backlog. Here's how:

   ✦ First list all the studies you have to finish. For example, write down the number of lessons you have to read, the homework you have to complete, etc.

   ✦ Now, number them in order of urgency and importance. Suppose you have to finish two lessons of History and three of Biology, and there is a History test next week. Which lessons must you study first? History of course! Give #1 to History and #2 to Biology. In this way, number all work you have to clear, depending on the urgency. Then start by completing the work at number 1, then move to number 2, 3, etc.

   ✦ Also, beside each topic, note approximately how much *time* you need to finish it. For example, for two History lessons how much time do you need? If you need four hours, note this beside it. Then spend four hours to finish your History lessons. In this way complete all other work.

   An example of how the above steps will look like on paper is given below:

   2. Study three lessons of Biology—5 hours
   1. Study two lessons of History—4hours
   3. Submit Practicals—2 hours
   4. Write notes of two Chemistry lessons—5 hours

   You may later re-write the above list by serial number; that is, at number 1 write History, at number 2 write Biology, and so on. By using such planned steps, you can easily clear your academic backlog without stress and strain.

4. **Ask friends for help, if necessary, but don't wait for help and make this another excuse!**

   If you have any problem in completing studies, don't hesitate to ask for help. To make friends help you faster, offer to help them solve some of their problems in which you are an expert. Find friends or classmates to exchange help.

   If possible, also ask teachers or parents to help you. However, don't wait for others' help. Till the help arrives, work to finish the next topic on your list.

   ∞

CHAPTER 24

4 Secrets to Public Speaking

1. ANYONE can learn to speak in public, including you!

You may say, "Public speaking? I don't want to become a politician. I have no intentions of giving a speech." Yet, you still need to learn to speak to in public.

There are big advantages of learning to speak in public. The *most important advantage*: if you can speak in public, *you can speak anywhere*.

By learning to speak in public you gain the confidence to speak:

- Before your teachers
- In class, while answering
- During viva voce
- At job interviews, and many other places.

So RESOLVE to learn this important skill. Believe in yourself. Think **"I can"**, and you will find it easy to speak confidently.

2. Start with two- or three-minute speeches on topics *you like most*.

First practise the art of speaking, at home. Stand before the mirror and speak for 2-3 minutes. In this short speech, mention who you are, what your dream is, and what you would gain by succeeding in studies and reaching career goals.

Then speak before your family and friends. Gradually spread your wings or tongue! And enjoy more speaking success.

You will never be afraid of speaking before others if you define public speaking as, *just a conversation with a large number friends.* Imagine the audience as a group of your friends. If you think in this manner, you will never be afraid to speak in public.

3. Use public speaking opportunities in school or college.

Grab every chance to speak in school or college. Answer questions in class, participate in debates and make brief speeches whenever possible. These actions help build confidence. Your teachers will also notice you.

Don't worry about mistakes. Just go ahead and speak. What prevents many from speaking in public is the fear of making mistakes and being ridiculed.

Well, this is one view. The other way of looking at mistakes, which helps you grow, is to see mistakes as *opportunities* to learn and succeed.

Why are you in school or college? *To learn skills and acquire knowledge.* What is the best way to learn any skill? By practising, making mistakes, and improving on mistakes. This is the **proven** way of learning and mastering *any* skill.

So use your student life to practise, make mistakes and correct them! Then you will emerge with rich knowledge and skills—and be able to *launch your career* with a BIG BANG!

4. Form a speech-cum-debate club with friends.

Form a friends' club to practise public speaking. This is another good method to sharpen speaking skills. This will also benefit your friends.

Meet regularly; say one hour a week. Even if you meet once a month, it will do. Start with two-minute speeches on topics that are mutually interesting. With growing confidence and the ability to express thoughts on your feet, increase the duration of the speech to three minutes, five minutes and so on.

To make meetings and speeches more challenging, learn to:
- Tell interesting stories
- Narrate funny jokes
- Sing motivational songs

These activities help you gain more confidence, with the added advantage of making speeches more entertaining!

However, remember an important point: **don't criticize or laugh at each others' mistakes.** Instead, give positive feedback to improve delivery, pronunciation, body language, etc.

∞

CHAPTER 25

7 Secrets to Excel in Exams and Tests

1. Banish fear of exams from the mind. It hinders good performance.

If there is one thing that makes life difficult for students it is fear of exams. Get rid of it, at once.

How? Change your outlook. Instead of fearing exams, *think that exams are good for you*. Think of all the benefits you gain by clearing exams.

Here are some **major benefits**. *Remember* these whenever you fear exams:

> **Major Benefits of Passing Exams:**
> + Acquiring educational qualifications
> + Chance for a better job or career
> + Boosting your self-respect
> + Gaining the respect of others
> + Becoming more confident
> + Cultivating habits of success

Keep adding more benefits to this list. You will be amazed at how good exams are for you. And you will soon start loving them!

2. Programme the brain to help you excel in exams by visualizing yourself answering all questions correctly in the exams and getting top grades.

You have already learnt about visualization in the chapter, *'8 Secrets to Programme Yourself for Success'*. Using this powerful visualization method, *programme your brain* to help you perform better.

A few days or weeks before the exams, practise this visualization exercise every night before sleeping:

+ Lie down comfortably in bed. Close your eyes, relax and take 3-4 deep breaths.

- Now visualize these scenes:

You are sitting in an exam hall **comfortably**. You are writing your exam paper coolly and **correctly**. Your pen is moving smoothly because you know all the answers. You are **cheerfully** submitting your perfect answer sheet at the end of the exam. Then you are holding a report card in your hand which shows 'A' grade or the percentage you want. You have succeeded! Be happy. See yourself jumping with **joy**.

What happens when you do the above exercise? Then you actually *train* your brain to perform better in exams. You ensure **mental practice** for your brain to work coolly and efficiently during exams!

Remember, exams are 99 per cent mental work and 1 per cent physical work. Yes, it is *your brain* that has to do more work during exams than your body.

So by visualization, you can **train** the brain for top performance in exams. Also, this helps increase confidence, remove exam fear, anxiety and other exam-related problems.

3. Use affirmations to be more confident.

You have learnt about affirmations in the chapter *'8 Secrets to Programme Yourself for Success'*. The affirmation method is a good technique to perform better in exams and also improves one's thoughts and attitude during exams.

A few days or weeks before the exams, repeat this affirmation daily:

> *I like exams. I have unlimited brainpower. Using my unlimited brainpower I can easily pass the exams with high scores.*

Learn this affirmation by heart and repeat it thrice after you wake up in the mornings and before going to bed, and also just before you receive the question paper in the exam hall.

By repeating such an affirmation, you gain two benefits which help improve your performance:

- It increases confidence.
- It helps you think positive thoughts and develop a better attitude towards exams.

4. Use ideas in this book, and those suggested by teachers, to excel in each subject.

To score high in exams, you have to perform well in every subject, as each contributes to your final total. Ask each teacher what would be the best method to prepare for their subjects.

Teachers are experts in their subjects, so they can help you better. Note down all these suggestions and follow them sincerely.

Also, use the ideas and secrets given in this book to excel in your exams and tests.

5. Practise solving questions by writing answers to 'expected' or 'model' questions.

Make time to write answers to expected or model questions. You can find such questions at the end of your textbook. Or you can use the questions asked by your teacher for this purpose. If you can't find model questions, make up your own questions.

The practice of solving questions is very important for academic success as it helps you:

- Prepare thoroughly for exams
- Write answers fast
- Answer any question fluently and quickly

In other words, the more questions you solve, the easier it becomes to excel in exams. The only way to master any skill is *practise, practise, practise*! There is no other way!

6. Within an allotted time, solve question papers of previous exams.

This is a secret that all good students use regularly.

When you solve questions of previous exams:

- You gain confidence and feel, 'If I can solve questions of the previous exam, I can also solve questions of the coming exam.'
- Your fear of exams decreases.

So don't wait. Get hold of question papers of previous exams and solve them.

7. Stay fit and healthy to help the brain function at optimum level.

Illness during exams can have negative consequences. Your preparation and revision will be adversely affected.

So follow these basic rules of good health and remain healthy during exams:

- Have a strong desire to be healthy and energetic.

- Eat a balanced diet. Also eat some raw vegetables and fruits with each meal to supply vitamins, minerals and enzymes to your body. This helps in better absorption and metabolism of the food you eat.
- Drink 8 glasses of pure water.
- Exercise for at least 30 minutes a day so that your blood is properly oxygenated and the brain gets its favourite food—oxygen.
- Sleep for eight hours. Also take a mini-break of five minutes after every 30 minutes of studies. And take a break of ten minutes after studying for two hours, especially after 'difficult' subjects.

Now, why not decide to be healthy and energetic every day of your life, instead of remaining healthy only during exams?

Yes, you can. Just *decide* and think of ONLY BEING HEALTHY. With repeated thoughts, your brain influences you to think and act in a way that keeps you in good health—all your life.

∞

CHAPTER 26

11 Secrets to Write Perfect Answers in Exams

1. **Make your examiner's job easy. Write neatly and clearly so the examiner easily understands your answers.**

    Irritating the examiner with bad handwriting results in lower score. Be kind to examiners! Remember, they have to evaluate many answer papers.

    Imagine yourself in their place. Imagine how you would feel if you had to *struggle* to understand what the students have written! How would you feel? Absolutely irritated.

    Would you give such papers full marks? NEVER! So ensure you write answers neatly and legibly.

    This will make the examiner's job easy, and s/he will be influenced to give you more marks.

2. **Watch your grammar! Correct grammar is like good music to the ears of the examiner!**

    Incorrect grammar is bad music that irritates and angers examiners. An angry examiner is not good for your success. So take care of your grammar. Write answers in grammatically correct sentences. This makes a good impression on the examiner.

    If your grammar is poor, improve it with these techniques:

    + Revise grammar rules. Do exercises given in your grammar book and practise writing correct sentences.
    + Daily, write a few paragraphs of some English story or text. While writing, notice how each sentence is constructed.
    + Loudly read a few paragraphs daily from English newspapers or any book and notice how each sentence is written.
    + Speak in English (or in the language in which you have to give the exams) with friends. Ask them to correct your mistakes.

    Use these techniques regularly, or at least during vacations, until your grammar and sentence-writing improves.

3. Watch your spellings! Check for capital letters.

We know this sounds silly. After all, we are taught these things in primary school. But remember, the examiner has never seen you before, especially if you are giving Board or competitive exams. Your examiner has no idea of how good or smart you are. The only way s/he knows is *through your answer paper.*

So even if you write full answers correctly but make spelling mistakes, your examiner will think you don't know the basics! This will create a poor impression.

Also, incorrect spellings could even change the meaning of what you want to say, influencing the examiner into deducting marks. So be careful about spellings and capital letters, especially in Language exams.

4. Write smartly! Don't use lengthy paragraphs.

Long paragraphs strain the eyes (and brain) of the examiner and make him unhappy. Use shorter paragraphs of four to five lines. Write only *one point or idea in one paragraph.* Then you will not end up writing long paragraphs.

Also, writing answers in shorter paragraphs helps organize thoughts and answer better. Moreover, the examiner will be able to check answers easily and know that you have covered all points in your answers.

This makes evaluation of your paper a pleasure. A pleased examiner usually showers good marks!

5. In writing, use headlines and sub-headlines.

Write answers with headlines and sub-headlines wherever possible. Underline them or use a colour pen, if this is allowed.

Then write answers in detail under those headlines or sub-headlines.

Writing headlines and sub-headlines, especially in essay-type answers, is important because they:

- Catch the attention of an examiner immediately
- Quickly reveal all the key points you have covered in the answer
- Make your answer look impressive.

All this helps the examiner check an answer paper quickly. As you have made your examiner's job easier, there is every chance s/he might reward you with more marks.

6. Write formulas, dates, and important names in a slightly bigger size than the other words.

This is a good trick to make your answers more attractive. But ensure you don't overdo it. When writing an answer that is two paragraphs long, make sure you write only 2 or 3 words in bigger size. Else your answer might look odd.

Or you can use an *alternate trick*: instead of a bigger size, simply underline *important* words, names or formulas. But do not underline dates and formulas. Write these in bigger size only.

Smart tricks like these give you a big advantage—they grab the examiner's attention quickly and *show* that you have covered all the important points. Don't forget, an examiner has to check many papers and is usually in a hurry. These tricks ensure you make your examiner's work easy.

But remember: you can use these tricks easily during exams *only* if you first practise them at home. So practise writing answers to model questions by using all tricks in this chapter.

7. When you have to give more than one example or multiple points, write them one below the other with serial numbers.

Don't ever forget this technique. Whenever you have to write answers in points or examples, always write each point or example one below the other. And number each one like this:

1. Your examiner will know immediately that you have covered all points.
2. You will not *forget* any point! As you write with serial numbers, you will know whether you covered all the examples or not. This in-built check ensures complete answers.
3. Your answer looks neat, creating a good impression on the examiner.

Thereby the chance of full marks increases.

8. Present answers in simple words and sentences.

Everyone loves to read simple English. Even the examiner! Besides, *you* will make fewer mistakes if you write in simple words and short sentences.

Also, the examiner will understand what you want to communicate instantly. As a result you stand a good chance of getting more marks without overloading your brain or that of the examiner!

So avoid long or complicated words and sentences.

9. When solving mathematical questions, pay attention to formulas, steps, and units.

You can easily score full marks in mathematics if you write answers properly.

To solve the maths paper perfectly, pay attention to:
- *Writing* solutions in proper steps. Don't skip any step, or you may not get full marks, even if the answer is correct.
- *Underlining* formulas, important steps, and final answers.
- *Checking* whether your answer is correct or not, *before* submitting the answer sheet.

With these simple steps, you can solve your maths problems properly, make the answer sheet look more attractive and score higher marks.

10. Keep the answer sheet as neat as possible. Avoid frequent corrections and overwriting.

It is hard to check an answer sheet filled with scratches, overwriting and frequent corrections.

Do your best to keep the answer sheet neat. You can achieve this more easily by:
- The visualization exercise given in the previous chapter '7 Secrets to Excel in Exams and Tests'.
- The practice of answering by solving model questions at home, before the exam begins.

With the above, you *train* the brain to write answers quickly and neatly.

Remember...

> *Your brain can do ANYTHING*
> *it is trained to do, and does nothing*
> *you do not train or expect it to do!*

11. An answer sheet is the ONLY medium to showcase your knowledge to the examiner.

Your answer sheet shows the examiner exactly how much you have learnt and what kind of student you are. So develop a *strong desire* to present answer papers neatly and accurately.

When you develop such a strong desire, you can do anything. As mentioned earlier, when you have a strong desire to achieve something *your brain helps you achieve it.*

Remember, checking your answer sheet should be a pleasure for the examiner. More pleasure results in more marks!

∞

CHAPTER 27

12 Secrets to Make Your Exam Day Perfect

1. Ensure *at least* six hours' sleep prior to the exam day. Eight hours sleep is even better to keep you fresh and alert.

You have already learnt about the importance of sleep and its effect on the brain. Scientists note that when we have proper rest and sleep, the brain works faster and more efficiently. *Concentration and memory power also increases*—so essential for top success in exams.

So sleep for eight hours before the exam day. Then you will concentrate better, recall answers quickly and write faster. If you can't sleep for eight hours, sleep for at least six hours.

You can avoid exam stress and sleep longer *if* you finish your preparations well before the exams. During exams, simply revise all the topics.

2. Eat light, nutritious food.

Eat well before going for exams and supply your body and mind with energy!

Eat food that is light and easily digestible. Usually a combination of carbohydrates, vegetables and proteins ensures good, long-lasting energy. Good examples of this combination are:

- *Roti* or *chapatti* and vegetable dishes
- *Rice-dal* with vegetables
- Cornflakes and milk with some dry fruits
- Bread sandwich with vegetables

If you are too nervous to eat, simple curd-rice will be good for your stomach. Or eat some bananas alongwith dry fruits like raisins and top this with a glass of milk.

However, don't eat fried or oily food as they are not easy to digest. Avoid sweets; they give instant energy but will soon leave you feeling low.

Finally, ensure you don't eat heavily before going for exams. It will make you drowsy. Also, never go on an empty stomach. The brain needs fuel to work.

If eating inside the exam hall is allowed, take some dry fruits that are rich in sugar—dates and raisins. Chew them slowly. They supply the brain with one of its favourite food—glucose.

3. **Be in positive mode. Before leaving home, do this visualization exercise for 3-5 minutes:**

   + Sit comfortably in a chair and close your eyes.
   + Breathe deeply and slowly 3-4 times. Then *imagine yourself* doing these things:

   You are leaving home **happily**. You have reached the exam hall **safely** with a smile on your face. You are sitting in the chair **comfortably**. You are writing the exam paper coolly and correctly. You are cheerfully submitting the perfect answer sheet at the end of the exam. Finally, you return home with a **big smile on your face**.

   Feels good, doesn't it? This exercise improves the mood instantly, makes your thoughts positive and calms you by reducing exam fear and stress.

   It also increases confidence. So do this visualization exercise before going for exams. It only takes a few minutes.

4. **Enter the exam hall with a smile. Don't bother about the result or your performance. Just do the job and keep your cool.**

   When you reach the exam hall, it is natural to feel the heart racing, a stomach full of butterflies, the neck and cheeks turning hot, and the hands sweating. All this is a sure sign of stress!

   Don't worry! Such feelings are your body's *natural response* to a challenge or fight. You cannot overcome these feelings *completely*.

   Besides, some degree of stress is indeed good for you as it **stimulates the brain and makes it more alert,** which helps you perform better in exams!

   So don't worry if you feel signs of stress. It is *good* for you. Ignore your pounding heart and enter the exam hall with a smile on your face. Say "Hi" to all your friends. Make some small talk, but don't discuss the exam. Divert your attention to other things until the exam begins.

   Always remember that your success in exams is *intimately linked* to how well you have learned to use your brain. And the key to efficient use of your brain is to **use the right thought to *trigger* the right neuronal network in your brain.**

   In short, the thought of failure NEVER helps you do better in exams. Instead, think of doing well in exams. This thought has more chances of activating the right neuronal networks in the brain where your answers have been recorded. So…

> **Think ONLY about what you desire to achieve, NEVER about what you don't want.** This is *the BIG secret* of success—in exams, career, and life.

All this will help you control stress, stay cool and finish your exam successfully.

What if you *still* feel so stressful that you can't think straight? Then use the next secret!

5. Sit comfortably on your chair, relax, and take 3-4 deep breaths.

This is very important. Don't forget this once you sit on your chair.

In the previous page, you learnt that some degree of stress is good. But excess stress can create problems. For example, if you feel you don't remember answers or cannot concentrate, or feel paralysed with fear or dizzy, you are probably under too much stress.

In such a situation, calm yourself by:

- Drinking some water. Always keep a bottle of water with you.
- Sitting straight and comfortably in your chair. Rest your feet properly on the ground. Don't curl your toes. And take 3 or 4 deep, slow breaths.
- *Not thinking about*: what kind of question paper you get, how you perform, what happens if you fail, and other bad thoughts.
- Telling yourself repeatedly, "I am cool. I am smart. I have unlimited brainpower. I remember everything. I can answer any question. *I am eager to write answers!*"

Now stop worrying and pay attention to the exam. You will soon feel better.

6. When you receive the exam paper, read the instructions and questions carefully.

You would love to zoom ahead and start solving questions quickly the moment you receive the question paper. But wait!

First read all instructions at the top of the question paper carefully. This ensures you don't miss important information. And before you write answers, read and understand each question properly. This ensures you don't misunderstand questions and write wrong answers!

All this may require you to spend an extra minute or two. But *do it*. Never skip these actions. Each year many students lose crucial marks either because they did not understand the question properly or did not read the instructions carefully.

Besides, these actions have an extra advantage: they tell the brain *what it has to do* in the exam, so that you can write correct answers within the time limit.

7. Answer the easy questions first, *if allowed*. Write neatly. Your first page must make a good impression on the examiner.

To score high, the first impression has to be *good*. The best way to do this is to keep your first page neat—by writing answers correctly and in good handwriting. Avoid overwriting on the first page.

You can do this without any problem, if you are *allowed* to answer easy questions first. Then start by solving the question whose answer you know *correctly*. You will not make mistakes then.

So, if allowed, choose your first question carefully and then go onto the next question that is easy. Attempt difficult questions in the end.

But don't worry if this is not allowed. Just do your best and write whatever you know in neat handwriting. Also try to keep the second and third page of your answer sheet neat. This makes more of an impression on the examiner.

This ability to write answers quickly yet neatly comes only if you practise *writing* answers to model questions at home, a few days before the exams.

8. If you forget some points, leave some blank space and start solving other questions.

If you forget some part of your answer, don't panic. Or you will get nervous and this will affect your confidence. You may even lose valuable time.

Don't think, "This happens to me all the time!" Or, "Why am I so dumb?" If you think negatively, you will require *more time* to recall information or may not even remember it. *What you think* affects your brain and memory power.

In such situations, ignore what you don't remember. Stay calm. Leave some space blank and start solving other questions. In the end, return to this and try to recall the rest of the answer. Don't be surprised if you now recall everything.

This is how the brain functions—when you forget something the brain keeps searching for it at a subconscious level, even while you are busy answering other questions!

So there is a higher chance you may remember answers at the second attempt.

9. Attempt all compulsory questions.

Don't leave compulsory questions unanswered. Or you will lose much marks.

If you don't remember answers to some compulsory questions, use these tricks:

- Answer such questions after you have solved all other questions.
- Even if you don't know or recall the answer completely, *write as much as you know*. If you leave the question blank, you get zero. But if you write something, you may get some marks that will add to your total.
- If you can't remember any direct points, write any related information. If this hits the mark, the examiner may reward you with some marks, which is better than zero!

Thereby, allow the brain to find answers to such questions. *Expect* your brain to give ideas to write answers. In this way, do your best to solve all questions within the time limit.

10. If you feel faint, uneasy or too tense during exams, take a mini-break and relax.

Sometimes, due to fear or tension we feel 'blanked out' or uneasy during exams.

If you feel this, don't panic but do the following:

- Stop writing immediately.
- Sit straight and comfortably in the chair. **Close your eyes** and take 4 to 5 slow, deep breaths. Then start breathing normally.
- Now, open your eyes and continue writing.

This mini-break helps you feel better.

Also drink water, if available. It is best if you keep a bottle of water with you during exams. Drinking water calms you.

Alternately, carry some chocolate and eat this if you feel uneasy. Sugar present in the chocolate provides energy and helps you feel better.

If you are still uneasy, ask the examiner for help.

11. **Finally, check whether you have answered all questions properly.**

Checking gives finishing touches to the answer sheet. It is the ultimate secret to make your answer sheet perfect.

So before submitting the answer sheet, check the following:

- First check whether you have answered all questions you were supposed to do and whether you have numbered them correctly.
- Check if you have left blank spaces to write answers you couldn't recall earlier. If so, try to recall and write them now.
- Check if you can add more points or information to any answer.
- Check for spelling mistakes.

To do all this, solve the exam paper quickly and save the last 10 to 15 minutes for checking.

12. **Always remember this Life-saving Tip: once you hand over the answer paper,** *stop worrying about the result. Just expect the best.*

Once you have submitted the answer paper, come out of the exam hall and forget about it. It's over!

Don't think about what you did write or didn't write. Don't worry whether you will get enough marks or not. Worrying:

- Drains mental energy.
- Decreases concentration and motivation.
- Increases fear and anxiety, making you depressed.

All this works against you. This might adversely affect your next paper.

So **never** worry if you haven't done well. You can't do anything about it. Now...

The result is not in your control.

So think only about how to do better in the next paper, and **expect the best.** NEVER FORGET this secret.

∞

CHAPTER 28

14 Secrets to Combat Stress

1. The best remedy: *avoid* **stressful situations!**

In the previous chapter we mentioned that some degree of stress is good. But too much stress can create problems. The best way to deal with excess stress: *avoid situations or actions that create stress.*

Generally, there are two main causes of stress:

- **Mismanagement of time:** Most students waste time at the start of the academic year. When the exams arrive, they scramble to finish studies. Result? Stress and anxiety. So the BEST remedy—study regularly, right from the day school or college begins.

- **Wrong thinking:** This usually involves comparisons with others and thinking, "I should get more marks than her." Or expecting too much from yourself. For example, "Last time I got 60%. This time I will score 95%." Avoid such thinking which increases stress. Aim to improve performance in practically possible stages.

2. Take the bull by the horns. Remove the causes of stress.

If you are caught in a situation where you feel stressed and anxious about studies or exams, what should you do?

Simple… take the bull by the horns. Identify the exact reason why you feel stressed and deal with it. For example:

- If you feel tense because you have not completed your studies, practicals or project, cancel all other activities, and start your work immediately. Use ideas given in the chapter, '4 Secrets to Clear Backlog Quickly'.

- If you fear exams, get rid of your fear by using secrets given in, '7 Secrets to Excel In Exams and Tests'.

- If you feel stressed because you constantly compare yourself with your classmates, stop doing this. You cannot control others' performance. You can only control *your performance.* So compare *your* performance with the previous performance and improve upon it by setting *realistic goals*. Tell yourself, "In the last exam I scored 75%. In the next exam I am going to score 80%."

3. **Walk for 30 minutes. Go alone or with a friend. Also discuss stressful feelings with your friend.**

Besides removing the cause of stress, also use other tricks to reduce stress.

Walking is one such simple trick that reduces stress. Walking:

- Improves oxygenation and blood circulation in the body, which makes you feel more fresh and energetic.
- Stimulates release of brain chemicals like endorphins that make you feel good and improves your mood positively.

Compared to other exercises, walking is simple. You don't need machines or equipment. So start walking for at least 30 minutes each day. Walking for 45 minutes or one hour is even better. Do a brisk walk or one at moderate speed, depending upon your fitness.

While walking, pay attention to things on the way and people around you. This diverts your mind toward other things and stops you from worring about problems. This helps reduce stress.

4. **When you are too tense, take a hot bath. Sleep for 8 to 10 hours.**

The traditional combination of a hot bath and good night's sleep also reduces stress.

Two good things happen when you take a hot bath: it increases blood circulation and helps muscles relax. These two changes improve your mood and thoughts!

After the bath, lie down in bed and try to sleep. Don't think about anything else.

To stop yourself thinking about problems or exams:

- Close your eyes. Take 3-4 slow, deep breaths. Loosen your body and relax.
- Focus the mind on your breathing, on the outward and inward movement of breath. This not only calms you, but also helps you sleep soundly.

Initially you may not find it easy to concentrate on your breathing. Don't worry. Whenever the mind wanders towards your problem, gently bring it back to focus on your breathing again. Within days, you will become adept at this.

5. Visit a friend's house. The one who has no exam! Talking with a friend will make you feel better.

Change of place or surrounding diverts attention from the tension. This helps reduce stress. So leave your study place and visit any good friend. If possible, visit a friend who has no exam. This ensures you do not end up talking about the exam!

Also, when you visit your friend, instead of telling him about your problem, inquire about his life. Just listen with genuine interest to your friend's response.

This diverts attention to something other than your problems or worries. You will start feeling better in a few minutes.

6. Go to a movie, museum, park, zoo, restaurant or anywhere else for some time to feel better.

This is another technique to give your brain a break. And stop thinking about exams and other problems.

Just concentrate on having fun. Go for a good, entertaining movie. Or walk through a museum, park, or zoo. Or simply hang around a coffee house or restaurant with friends or any family member. Then you will be able to return to your studies with fresh energy.

But if you don't have any nice, entertaining places near your home, don't worry. You can find the most pleasant places right inside your head!

Sit in your garden, front yard or on the terrace. Close your eyes and visualize yourself enjoying at a beautiful place that has everything you can ever imagine to see, touch, feel, and enjoy. It could be a beautiful forest or garden or mountain or even a Disneyland! Just imagine yourself running around and enjoying.

This fun, relaxing mental visualization calms you and provides relief from stress. So let imagination run loose and wipe out that tension from your mind.

7. Exercise, jog, hike, swim, do anything you like. Physical activity is a good way to burn stress.

Exercise is a powerful stress-buster. Like walking, other physical exercises also help you get rid of stress. If you are bored of walking everyday, you could do any other exercise: yoga, aerobics, cycling, jogging, swimming, hiking, playing tennis, football, badminton, table tennis, etc. Or you can join a gym.

Simply choose an exercise that feels comfortable. Also ensure you *like* the exercise. Merely doing an exercise does not give you much benefit. But when you *enjoy* the exercise, you gain all the advantages:

✦ You get faster results.

- ✦ Brain chemicals or neurotransmitters like endorphins are released more easily, making you feel much better.
- ✦ You feel more peaceful and stress decreases more quickly.

So for quick relief, choose an exercise you enjoy and do it regularly.

8. **If you are a bookworm, read your favourite book or some novel *with a happy ending*. It will improve your mood.**

This is another good method to reduce stress, if you are a book lover. Reading being a mental activity, it diverts the mind away from problems, worries or exam fears.

But for full advantage, select a proper book such as:

- ✦ Motivational books that encourage you and lift your mood.
- ✦ Funny stories or novels that ensure a good laugh.
- ✦ Any book that has a gripping tale with a *happy ending*.

Don't read books with tragic endings or too much tension. Remember, you are reading to improve your mood and relax!

9. **If you have a pet, play with it to feel better.**

Studies show that playing with pets reduces stress. It even helps fight off problems like depression, loneliness and blood pressure.

When you play with pets like dogs and cats, you activate emotions of love, affection, and laughter. These powerful emotions help to change your body chemistry positively and make you calm, happy and relaxed.

What's more, you can talk to pets endlessly and they do not answer back or talk about your exams! So snuggle up with your pet. Play with it, run around or go for a walk.

10. **Visist places of worship and unburden yourself with God! You will feel lighter.**

For centuries, people have known the power of prayer. Now even scientists agree that praying reduces tension, helps one feel calm and gives courage to face difficult situations.

So if you believe in God, pray for relief from your stressful condition. Pray at home whenever you like. Be thankful to God for all the good in your life. And ask the Almighty to *always* be at your side and give you the strength to succeed in exams!

Visit the temple or place of worship. Sit quietly for some time and let the atmosphere of spirituality and calmness soothe your mind.

11. Meditate for 15 minutes. During meditation, visualize yourself sitting at any peaceful place. This relaxes and beats stress.

Meditation is another well-recognized method to relieve stress, tension, and depression. So use this simple, powerful method regularly. Even meditating for 15 minutes daily helps immensely.

Here is how you meditate:

- **First, relax:** Lie down in your bed or sit comfortably in the chair. Or sit cross-legged on the floor using a mat. Then close your eyes. Take 3-4 slow, deep breaths. While exhaling, relax. Then start breathing normally. Now, begin meditating using any of the two methods given below:
- **Breathing method:** This is an ancient method based on yoga. All you have to do in this method is *pay attention* to the outward and inward movement of your breath. Keep your mind focused on it. Feel the air going in and out of your nostril. If you start thinking about something else, don't worry. Gently bring your attention back to the breathing again.
- **Visualization method:** Mentally imagine or visualize yourself walking in a cool, calm place. It could be your garden, some beautiful place near a river or anywhere else you like. Forget all troubles and imagine yourself relaxing.

Slowly open your eyes and come out of meditation. You will feel refreshed and cheerful.

12. Help a friend or classmate experiencing a similar condition!

This is a smart trick to beat stress. When you help others, you automatically shift attention from your problems to the other's problems.

Also, you now think differently. Instead of thinking about problems, you think about *ideas* to solve your friend's problem and make him happy.

And a big secret: when you ensure happiness for others, you also become happy. Also, you then become aware of ways to solve *your* problems. This is a win-win method to beat stress.

13. You can discuss problems with parents or a friendly teacher.

Always tell parents what's bothering you. They will certainly help and suggest ways to deal with it.

If you feel uncomfortable talking to your parents about the problem directly, use indirect ways. Put this across as your friend's problem. For example, "My friend is afraid she might fail. What should she do to stop feeling afraid?"

You can also ask a friendly teacher advice. For example, ask your teacher to explain difficult topics or how to prepare better for such exams.

In this way, seek help from others and make your academic success easier—without stress.

14. If you still find it hard to handle stress, go to a counsellor. Or send us an email!

If all these things do not work, seek professional help from a counsellor or doctor. Don't avoid it. Too much stress for a long period can be harmful. Remember, there is a solution for ALL problems. You just have to *find* this.

At the end of this book, you will find details about our website www.mindpowerguide.biz. Visit this for our email address and write to us for additional help to handle stress, if you desire.

Or just use the free information and articles on the website to know yourself better. Remember: *the more you know yourself, the easier it becomes to solve your problems or to prevent them.*

∞

CHAPTER 29

11 Secrets to Prevent Problems

1. Keep your documents like an ID card, admission card and other records in a safe place.

This is the best method to avoid problems during exams or any other time. Keeping things in an *organized way* prevents dreadful situations.

Imagine not finding your admission card on the morning of the exam! You will be upset, may be late for the exam and enter the hall upset or angry. This can badly affect your performance.

So keep all documents in a safe place. And remember where you have kept them! Check periodically to see whether those things are still there.

Also, tell your parents where you have kept them. They can remind you if you forget. *Prevention is always better than cure.*

2. Keep your notes and books safely.

Notes and textbooks are your most important possessions, at least till the exams are over! So keep them safely.

Some tips to help you:

- Organize notes and textbooks neatly in a bookshelf or drawer. And keep it locked when not in use.
- Once you finish reading your notes or textbook, put them back in place. If you leave them lying around, these might get misplaced.
- If you have to lend notes or textbooks to a classmate, ensure the classmate is trustworthy and has a reputation for returning things! Also, you must know where your classmate lives. In case your notes are not returned on time, you can get this back personally.

3. Check the school notice board periodically for announcements on events or programmes.	**I**magine walking into school and discovering that the last date to submit the final practical copy is today! To avoid such unpleasant surprises, read the notice board regularly. If you have been absent from school for some time, ring a friend and check if any announcement was made during your absence. This will help you avoid unpleasant surprises when you return to class. Finally, make it a habit of submitting homework, assignments or projects well before the due date.
4. Display your exam timetable on the wall near your desk. Note the dates and timings carefully.	**T**his is every student's nightmare: studying the entire night for the maths exam, then walking into class the next day to find it is an English exam! To prevent such a nightmare, here are some time-tested remedies: ♦ Note the dates and timings of the exam carefully. ♦ Then copy the timetable on another paper at home. Paste this on the wall near your table. You can now refer to the timetable easily and avoid making any mistake. ♦ Crosscheck your exam timetable with other classmates. This ensures you have not made any mistake while copying it.
5. Be nice to classmates, office staff, teachers and everyone else!	**A**lmost all successful people use a secret that helps them beat any problem and achieve success faster. It is called "Connection". If you have *connections with important people*, you can find help in any situation and thus achieve success effortlessly. So develop the habit of maintaining good relations and connections with people who are important for your success. The important people for your success are the school or college staff, teachers and classmates. So maintain good relations with them. Be nice, talk politely and avoid arguments with them. Thereby, they will *remember* you as a good human being. Whenever you need help or guidance, they will help you readily! Use this secret in all areas of life: career, personal or social. Make it a lifelong policy to maintain good relations with everyone.

6. Keep safe distance from notorious students inclined toward violence, alcohol, drugs, etc.

Remember the saying, 'One rotten apple spoils others in the basket.' When we mix with people who have bad habits, we tend to become like them. Such people try to *influence* us to follow their bad habits.

For example, a student who drinks tells his friends that 'the occasional drink doesn't hurt'. What he doesn't mention is that the moment you pick up the glass for the first time, you break *your resistance* to that habit. Once you break the initial resistance, it is very easy to break it repeatedly. In other words, 'occasional' drinking soon turns into 'regular' bouts.

Stay away from notorious students. Don't invite them to your home and don't visit their home.

Keep the company of *good students*. Good company protects you from bad habits.

7. NEVER fall in love during your student years.

This sounds like a heart breaker. But love can wipe out your concentration in nanoseconds. The result? POOR GRADES! If you face this temptation, ask yourself, "Will this ensure top grades?" **NO!**

If you want proof of how love ruins academic success and future prospects, just check the daily newspapers. You will read lots of stories about how untimely love affairs have ruined many young lives.

Don't let your life become such NEWS!

Never say 'yes' to offers of love when you are still in school or college. If the suitor persists, ask that 'lovely' person to renew the offer *after* you firmly settle down in your career or profession...

*And **not a day before that!***

Student life is the foundation of your whole life. Use it wisely. Then you will enjoy more happiness, success and wealth for the rest of your life.

8. Take good care of your health during exams. Avoid junk food. Exercise. Relax. Sleep well. Drink 8 glasses of water daily.

Two things are important to succeed in exams: good study preparation and good health. Most students pay attention to studies, but ignore their health!

We had a student in our workshop who once narrated a sad experience. She had studied well for her 12th standard Board exams. But when the exams began, she suddenly fell ill and could not sit for three papers. She lost one year.

To prevent such a tragedy follow these tips:

- Take good care of your health months before the exam begins.
- Don't eat and drink outside. Eat home-cooked meals. If this is not possible, eat only where good quality food is served. Avoid junk food.
- Eat and sleep at the same time everyday. Irregular eating and sleeping weakens the digestive and immune system.
- Drink plenty of water. Relax and exercise everyday for at least 30 minutes.

9. **Keep a checklist. Check whether you have packed everything you need for the exams: ID card, pen, pencil, eraser, sharpener, ruler, calculator, chocolates, etc.**

Most students pack their things on the exam day, right before leaving home. This is a risky habit, as you might forget something in a hurry. Always pack your bag on the night before the exam.

In fact, prepare a list of everything you need, *two days before the exam begins*. Note everything you need: Identity Card, pen, pencil, colour pens, eraser, sharpener, ruler, calculator, chocolates, etc.

The night before the exams, check the list and pack everything in your bag. If you remember anything extra, add that too in your bag.

10. **Never lose faith in yourself. Treat setbacks as learning experiences.**

Despite best efforts, sometimes things go wrong. If they do, don't lose faith in yourself. Don't think it is the end.

Studies and exams are important, no doubt. But life is *more* important! WHY are you studying?

To lead a better, more successful life

So keep this big picture of life in mind always. Studies are just one step toward that better life.

So if you perform poorly or something else goes wrong, don't get depressed. And don't ever think of jumping into a lake!

If you score less marks, analyse what went wrong. Find out your mistakes. Then correct these and prepare better the next time.

If you score a low percentage and don't get admission in medical, engineering or another course you desire, find an alternate career. Then begin studying for it. There are various ways to achieve success in life. If one way doesn't work, try another. The important thing: **don't give up. Then nothing can stop you!**

11. Always keep important phone numbers handy.

Numbers of parents, friends, counsellor, doctor, and any other person close to you should always be handy. You never know when you might need help. So keep such phone numbers in your purse, bag or wallet or store them in your mobile.

When in trouble, *control* the mind and get help faster by:

- Staying calm. Don't panic. And *expect help to arrive.* Continue to expect help until you get it.
- Believe it or not, your brain can **attract** help faster when you *expect* you will get help soon, **not** when you are in a doubtful or anxious mode. When doubtful or afraid, your trouble might actually increase!

Always remember this secret in emergencies: stay calm and expect help to arrive.

∞

CHAPTER 30

6 Master Secrets to be More Successful

1. To overcome weakness, draw strength from your success. List all achievements, small or big, and remember them.

Success breeds success. To overcome weakness or fear, derive strength from your past successes and achievements. Here's how:

+ Prepare a Success List by noting all your achievements—small or big (as explained in the chapter '6 Secrets to Boost Confidence').

+ Now read your past achievements and remember 'that feeling' of achieving success, 'that feeling' of doing things excellently. *Transfer this feeling* to studies; you will feel more confident and perform better. For example, if you are good at painting, tell yourself, "If I am good at one thing, I can be good at others too. If I can paint well, I can study well too."

+ Mentally praise yourself frequently for all your achievements.

2. Whether work or studies, *do it just because you have to do it*.

"Studying is tough." "Studying is good." "Studying is boring." What do these sentences indicate? They indicate different attitudes about studying.

Studying is just studying. It's neither easy nor hard. It is something we have to do to acquire knowledge and pass the exams. But our attitude makes us attach different labels such as "boring," "difficult," "important," etc.

But successful students do not label their studies. They merely see studying as a ticket to a prosperous career and study regularly to achieve their goal. So be smart and follow successful students.

Put aside all likes and dislikes, all bad moods and negative opinions. Study because you *have to study*. Do it *just because you have to do it*. There is no other option.

This is a powerful secret that will also help you in your future career: *do your work everyday, just because you have to do it, irrespective of whether you like it or not, whether you feel in the mood or not. Then you will achieve more success in your career and in life.*

3. Cultivate and develop the reading habit.

There is a popular saying: 'Today's readers are tomorrow's leaders'.

Reading gives you immense power and advantage. Here's how:

- *Reading stretches the boundaries of your mind.* It fires your imagination and gives you new ideas and solutions to problems.
- *Reading gives knowledge and information—**throughout life**.* Reading doesn't end with college. You need to keep in touch with the latest developments by reading. You can improve yourself at any age by reading positive information.
- *Reading gives you an edge over competitors.* By regularly reading about new concepts, and developments related to your career, you can beat competitors and get ahead in your career faster!
- *Reading helps you learn new skills.* Right now, as you read this book, you are learning new skills and tricks to achieve more success in studies. Similarly, read other books to learn skills related to your career.

4. Cultivate a positive attitude and maintain this. Always.

There are many advantages in having a positive attitude in life. A positive attitude is the only way to see the *useful side* in every situation. Without this, no one can achieve big success.

For example, students who think education is useless will fail or score low. Whereas students who think education leads to rich living will pass exams with a high score and land themselves in promising jobs or career.

Besides, a positive attitude helps you *find more opportunities*. Thereby you achieve greater success.

Conversely, people with a negative attitude usually spend their time criticizing everything—their life, surroundings, society and government. Such people fail to notice good opportunities around them.

Furthermore, a positive attitude keeps you healthy and cheerful, which is so essential for success.

So be wise. Make full use of the power of a positive attitude—first by cultivating it, then by applying it in every situation in your life.

5. Learn to use computers.

Nowadays, computers are needed everywhere. The skill of using computers can help you in studies and your career.

There are many student-related websites such as www.mindpowerguide.biz where you will find information on study success and self-improvement.

As far as a career is concerned, MS-Office, Tally, DTP, etc. are some of the popular short-term courses that are useful in computer related jobs.

If interested in working exclusively with computers, you can learn courses like C, C++, HTML, Java, PHP, MySql, etc. that will help you find jobs as a software developer or web designer.

Even if you don't want a career related to computers, join some crash course to learn the basics of computers and the Internet. Today, the Internet has become a good source of information.

Also, many daily activities like chatting, shopping, booking train or air tickets, and banking are being done via computers and the Internet. So learn computers to stay in tune with changing times.

6. Use methods in this book till you reach the goal.

You can achieve the results you want *only* when you take planned, intelligent action. Methods given in this book help you think and act intelligently—to reach your chosen goal.

Here is a secret formula for greater success in Education, Career, Personal and Social Life:

LBTB ⟶ MBTB = Guaranteed Success

Performance **L**ittle **B**etter **T**han **B**efore leads to performance **M**uch **B**etter **T**han **B**efore, which **G**uarantees **S**uccess.

Anyone can do anything just *a little better than before*! This consistent 'little' improvement **accumulates** into much bigger improvements. This is how champions and world-famous people are born. You can also do it.

Just *use* the ideas in this book to improve yourself, little by little everyday. Within no time, you will be transformed into a new powerful person for whom everything is possible.

Wish You Great Success!

∞

www.ingramcontent.com/pod-product-compliance
Lightning Source LLC
Chambersburg PA
CBHW080552230426
43663CB00015B/2813